EMPOWERED!

EMPOWERED!
¡EMPODERADOS!

LATINOS
TRANSFORMING
ARIZONA POLITICS

LISA MAGAÑA AND CÉSAR S. SILVA

THE UNIVERSITY OF
ARIZONA PRESS

TUCSON

The University of Arizona Press
www.uapress.arizona.edu

ISBN-13: 978-0-8165-4224-6 (paperback)

Cover design by Nathaniel Roy, Notch Design
Art direction by Derek Thornton, Notch Design
Cover image courtesy of Shutterstock
Texture image courtesy of Alamy
Typeset by Sara Thaxton in 10.25/15 Minion Pro (text), Abolition, and Proxima Nova (display)

Library of Congress Cataloging-in-Publication Data
Names: Magaña, Lisa, author. | Silva, César S., 1982– author.
Title: Empowered! : Latinos transforming Arizona politics / Lisa Magaña and César S. Silva.
Description: Tucson : The University of Arizona Press, 2021. | Includes bibliographical references and
    index.
Identifiers: LCCN 2020044702 | ISBN 9780816542246 (paperback)
Subjects: LCSH: Mexican Americans—Arizona—Politics and government—21st century. | Hispanic
    Americans—Arizona—Politics and government—21st century. | Political participation—Arizona.
Classification: LCC F820.M5 M34 2021 | DDC 979.100468/72—dc23
LC record available at https://lccn.loc.gov/2020044702

Printed in the United States of America
♾ This paper meets the requirements of ANSI/NISO Z39.48-1992 (Permanence of Paper).

CONTENTS

ACKNOWLEDGMENTS

This book could not have been completed without the assistance and support of numerous people. First, I'd like to thank my co-author, César S. Silva, for your insightful research and writing on this subject. I think our book is going to make an important contribution to the study of Arizona, Latinos, immigration, and politics. I'd also like to acknowledge my colleagues at the School of Transborder Studies at Arizona State University. We live in Arizona at an extraordinary time, and I value your collegiality. I especially want to thank the reviewers and individuals who provided valued feedback and recommendations on the manuscript, especially Irasema Coronado, Christine Marie Sierra, and Tony Payan.

I am most grateful to Clara Moffitt, an excellent researcher, writer, and organizer. I was so lucky to work with Clara on this project and so proud and happy for all of her accomplishments. I would also like to thank the wonderful staff at University of Arizona Press: Kristen Buckles, Amanda Krause, Elizabeth Wilder, and Emily Shelton. On a personal note, I would like to thank some of my dear friends, especially Cecilia Menjívar, Tracey McAbee, and Eileen Diaz McConnell. Finally, I'd like to thank my family: Robert Short, Isabella Magaña, and Sofia Magaña.

Lisa Magaña

Words cannot express enough thanks or the amount of appreciation that I have for Dr. Magaña, who helped me through this process step by step.

Had it not been for her guidance and belief in my abilities, I would not have attempted such a feat in my young years. Thank you, Dr. Magaña, for allowing me to join you in the process of writing this book and for teaching me so much.

I am particularly grateful to Dr. Coronado for the advice and wisdom shared with me throughout the process of this book. Thank you for advocating for my success in all of my academic and teaching endeavors.

Thank you to my mother, of course. Had it not been for your sacrifices, I would not be here today. You will never truly know how much you have shaped me through your strength and unconditional love. *Gracias, mamá.*

Finally, the completion of this book could not have been accomplished without the support and patience of my family and loved ones. Thank you for understanding the importance of this book and for the sacrifices made to ensure that it would be completed. *Gracias por todo, mis amores.*

César S. Silva

EMPOWERED!

Introduction

Latino Politics

This book is about the latest phase of Latino politics in Arizona. Latinos have a long history of resistance to colonization, discrimination, and repatriation. Despite Arizona once being part of México, a number of pivotal events, legislation, and forces have aimed at limiting the full political participation of Latinos in the state. In this book, "politics" does not refer to simply voting; here, we use the term "politics" to mean "mobilizing change." Counterintuitively, when examining recent Latino political mobilization strategies, it appears that the more obstacles that have been placed to limit full political participation, the more powerful Latinos have become to resist those forces. This book highlights some innovative, inspiring, and successful mobilization strategies for increasing the political participation of Latinos in Arizona as well as other states where the Latino population is growing.

Historically, there has been a major political backlash by a wide range of traditional and nontraditional political players to the decades-long wave of anti-immigrant and, more generally, anti-Latino proposals. The traditional power players among Latinos include a mix of new and long-standing elected officials and community leaders, while nontraditional constituencies include high school students, working-class Latino voters, church members, and a diverse array of grassroots organizations.

Perhaps the most innovative among the political actors in Arizona are the immigrant activists. These brave and remarkable individuals have worked with others to, for instance, oust a state senate member, defeat a controversial sheriff, and elect candidates that believe in comprehensive immigration reform. These individuals, some of them university students, ask their allies to vote because they themselves cannot.

Another fascinating outcome of Latino politics in Arizona is that grassroots activists have become prominent players. Starting at the grassroots level, several of these political players have worked for mayors, city council members, and congressional members, as well as on gubernatorial and presidential campaigns.

Why Latinos and Arizona?

There are more than 329.2 million people living in the United States, and, as of 2019, 59.9 million people are of Hispanic origin; another 2.861 million people live in the U.S. Commonwealth of Puerto Rico. The close proximity to México and Central America makes the United States a prime destination for Latin American immigration. As a result, if Latinos in the United States had their own country, it would be the third largest Latin American population in the world, after México (U.S. Census 2020).

In 2000, the Census Bureau found that Latinos in the United States became the largest minority group, exceeding the African American population. The census also predicts that the Latino population will reach 129 million by 2060 and make up 31 percent of the nation's total population (Pew 2016). Not surprisingly, two-thirds of all Latinos in the United States are of Mexican origin, and, of that, 31 percent are foreign born. In Arizona, 63 percent of the state's population is predominately white, 23 percent is Hispanic or Latino, 4 percent Black, and the remaining Asian, Native Hawaiian or two or more races.

Although this book examines Latino politics in Arizona generally, the focus is predominately on the Phoenix metropolitan area, one of the fastest-growing counties in the United States. In 2020, the population of Arizona was 7,279,000, with more than half of the state's inhabitants living in Maricopa County or the Phoenix metropolitan area (4,485,000). In fact, Mar-

RACE AND ETHNICITY IN ARIZONA

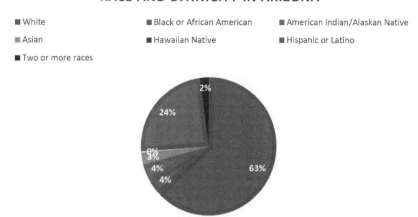

■ White   ■ Black or African American   ■ American Indian/Alaskan Native

■ Asian   ■ Hawaiian Native   ■ Hispanic or Latino

■ Two or more races

FIGURE 1 Race and ethnicity in Arizona. Source: https://www.census.gov /quickfacts/AZ.

TABLE 1 Race and ethnicity in Arizona

Race	Percentage
White	82.8%
Black or African American	5.1%
American Indian/Alaskan Naïve	5.3%
Asian	3.7%
Hawaiian Native	.3%
Hispanic or Latino	31.6%
Two or more races	2.9%

Source: U.S. Census, 2019

icopa is the fourth largest Hispanic county (1,380,000) in the United States, and Latinos make up 31 percent of the county's overall population (U.S. Census 2020). As could be expected, 90 percent of all Latinos in Arizona are of Mexican origin and are U.S. citizens.

Despite the narrative that Arizona has a large proportion of unauthorized immigrants, this is not the case. According to the Migration Policy Institute, there are approximately 226,000 unauthorized immigrants in the state.

TABLE 2 Total U.S. population of Hispanic/Mexican origin

Total U.S. population	329,200,000
Total Hispanic origin	59,900,000
Total Mexican origin	62%
Total foreign-born Mexican origin	31%

Source: U.S. Census, 2020

TABLE 3 Total Arizona Mexican origin and unauthorized population

Total Arizona population	7,279,000
Total Maricopa County	4,485,000
Total Hispanic Maricopa County	1,380,000
Total Mexican Origin in Maricopa County	90%
Total unauthorized	226,000

Source: U.S. Census, 2020

Researchers estimate that there has been a decrease of 70,000 unauthorized individuals since 2009, when there was an economic recession.

Over previous decades, the population in Arizona grew more than three times as fast as the rest of the nation. Between 1990 and 2010, Arizona Latinos more than doubled their numbers. Among the reasons for the Latino population boom were immigration, primarily from México and Latin America, and the demographic shift of U.S. Latino births, which have made Arizona one of the fastest-growing states in the country. Most recently, economic development and job opportunities have encouraged migration; many Latinos both native and undocumented have come to Arizona from other states seeking new opportunities.

Furthermore, Latino immigrants to Arizona have traditionally originated in northern Mexican states such as Chihuahua or Sonora. However, in recent years, Mexicans from the central and southern regions of México have become more visible. In the past decade, sustained political conflict and poor economic conditions in México's southern states have created an optimal situation for emigration (Díaz McConnell and Skeen 2009).

For Latino immigrants, Arizona provides opportunities that are harder to find in California, such as employment and affordable housing. Because metropolitan Phoenix is relatively new and spatially spread out, it lacks a compact immigrant community, such as San Francisco's Chinatown. Latinos live in neighborhoods scattered throughout the metropolitan area. These concentrations host a mixture of new Latino immigrants who have been able to find affordable housing, even given their generally low-paying jobs. Although both suburbs and more densely populated areas of the city have become home for new Latino immigrants, many of them are dispersed throughout poor neighborhoods (Menjívar and Magaña 2009).

Latinos are a relatively young group. Nationally, 81 percent of Latinos are under thirty-five years old. In an analysis of Census data by Stateline, an initiative of the Pew Charitable Trusts, it was found that Arizona had the largest racial generation gap. What this means for Arizona is that for ages sixty-five and older, minorities made up 18 percent of that population, while they made up 59 percent of the population under the age of eighteen (Wiltz 2015). In addition, nationally, 80 percent of seniors are white, while approximately 50 percent of people younger than eighteen years old are persons of color. In Arizona, this trend holds true, with the median age of the white, non-Hispanic population being forty-five years old, while the Latino median age is twenty-five (2015).

William Hart of the Morrison Institute has declared this demographic gap one of the most important issues facing Arizona right now: "America is and Arizona is dividing up into what they call the brown and the gray. . . . The older people who tend to be non-Hispanic whites tend to be higher educated, tend to be wealthier and more politically active and the Brown Latinos, who are significantly younger, will soon be the majority of the population" (Macias 2015).

TABLE 4 Latino eligible voters in Arizona

Total population, Arizona	7,279,000
Total eligible voters	5,042,000
Latino population	2,267,000
Latino eligible voters	1,188,000
Latino total population share	31.6%
Latino eligible voter share	23.6%

Source: Pew Research Center, "Mapping the Latino Electorate," 2020, https://www.pewresearch.org/hispanic/interactives/mapping-the-latino-electorate/iframe/ (accessed November 10, 2020).

In terms of electoral power, nationally a record thirty-two million Latinos are eligible to vote in the 2020 presidential election. In Arizona, one-third of Latinos are eligible to vote in the election, and these numbers have been predicted to increase.

Latino Politics in Arizona

For Latinos, protest politics has played a consistent role in mobilizing the community. Immediately after the annexation of the Southwest, newly identified Mexican Americans in Arizona were quick to organize against Anglo settlers who stole land and manipulated the legal system to cheat and disenfranchise the community. With the signing of the Treaty of Guadalupe Hidalgo in 1848, former Mexican citizens in the new U.S. territories were almost immediately relegated to second-class status. These new Mexican Americans fought back against the unfair policies and politics (Magaña and Mejia 2004).

The next period of Latino politics occurred over the first three decades of the twentieth century. Mexicans fleeing the repressive policies of the Porfirio Díaz administration openly opposed injustice in the United States and México. Until the early 1900s, immigration from México was virtually unrestricted. During the Mexican Revolution (1910–20), hundreds of thousands of Mexicans fled north to escape the violence of the war and the coinciding economic chaos. This event was the only discernible wave of solely Mexican immigration, and most of these immigrants settled in Los Angeles. Since that time, the immigration of Mexicans, unlike other groups, has been ongoing.

Interestingly, during this period mutualistas, or immigrant organizations, were formed to support newly arrived immigrants, while at the same time the mutualistas and immigrants that they served kept up to date with the politics in México. These were the first transnational organizations associated with Latino politics. Furthermore, several of these mutualistas have served as the foundation for Latino lobby and advocacy groups today (Moore and Pachon 1985).

The next significant period in Latino politics was in the 1940s, when Latinos worked steadily to engage further in traditional forms of electoral politics. Some Latino elected officials began their political careers around this time. Also, participation in World War II meant that Latino servicemen saw other parts of the world, which eventually resulted in their own migration out of poorer communities and into better living conditions. The GI Bill, a financial reward after participating in the armed services, resulted in some Latinos pursuing higher education, thereby moving out of poor communities and creating new generations of scholars (Rosales 2011).

During the 1960s and the early 1970s, mass civil rights demonstrations characterized Latino political engagement. Students, farm workers, and community leaders worked toward the elimination of racial inequalities in public schools, the workplace, and judicial and political systems. After these social movements, some activists began to work in more traditional and electoral political structures (Rosales 1997).

By the 1990s, the pace of Latino population growth was fueling further traditional political activity, including greater involvement by the community in major voter registration and voting turnout drives. Dozens of Latinos ran for office. In the process of political incorporation, Latinos were redefining notions of citizenship, community, and social rights, demanding inclusion and meaningful political participation (Hardy-Fanta and Gerson 2002). The 1990s also saw a growing connection between immigration, Latinos, and politics. In California, the controversial "Save Our State" initiative—better known as Proposition 187—was passed; this was one of the first laws linked to more punitive efforts to decrease unlawful immigration. With it, citizens of California attempted to deny social services, including education or welfare, to unauthorized immigrants. Ultimately, the initiative was found to be unlawful, but it set the stage for similar types of legislation in Arizona (Santa Ana 2002).

A visible shift in Latino politics came in the mid-2000s. Not coincidentally, this occurred at the same time that a number of anti-immigrant proposals were created. At this point, a growing movement made up of grassroots and traditional Latino political players organized to oppose anti-immigrant legislation. It was also during this period that Latino politics became more pan-Latino—that is, Latinos from groups other than Mexican galvanized and mobilized in order to confront the anti-immigrant sentiment (Magaña and Lee 2013).

In addition, Arizona became ground zero for the nation's debate over immigration policy and the role of American Latinos on the national political landscape. It is important to note that *all immigration-related laws are created at the federal level.* However, Arizona has straddled the line between what is immigration-related and what is, say, business-, education-, or election-related. For example, Arizonans passed a law stipulating that if you are an unauthorized immigrant student and have lived in the state for decades, the student is still required to pay out-of-state tuition to attend the university. Policy makers have insisted that this policy was not created to punish unauthorized students—rather, that universities have the right to require that they pay (Ryman and González 2017).

Arizona is the only state that has its own employer sanctions law. There is also a federal employer sanctions law that was passed in 1986 as part of the Immigration Reform and Control Act (IRCA). However, Arizonans wanted to make it especially tough on employers that knowingly hire unauthorized immigrants. The law was challenged at the federal level; although the Supreme Court saw it as an immigration-related issue, they ultimately ruled that the state could, in fact, require businesses to hire "legal" immigrants (Smith 2011).

In 2004, Arizona passed a law that citizens were required to show proof of citizenship when voting; a voter identification card was no longer sufficient. The rationale was that too many unauthorized immigrants were fraudulently voting, despite a lack of evidence of this taking place. Although the law was challenged and viewed as the state once again trying to address immigration-related issues, the courts ruled that it was not an immigration issue but rather a voting issue (Berman 2016). This policy was particularly tough on the elderly and on Native Americans who could not provide sufficient documentation. The courts have seen this particular policy as a violation of the Voting Rights Act (VRA).

Studies show that Latinos interpret anti-immigrant rhetoric as anti-Latino. Arizona has also muddled the narrative of what are immigration-related agendas and what are interpreted by many as ostensibly anti-Latino agendas. It is a miscalculation on the part of candidates to pander to an anti-immigrant agenda. One study has showed that, in areas with a growing Latino base, anti-immigrant agendas only served to mobilize Latinos to vote to defeat these candidates. In another study, the "Mexicans are rapists" comments by President Trump when he announced his candidacy also served to galvanize Latino voters (Newman, Shah, and Collingwood 2018). Furthermore, anti-immigrant agendas have not only energized Arizona's

Latino community, but also its non-Latino allies both across the state and nationwide (Nuño-Pérez 2018).

There are obvious demographic reasons to explain why immigration agendas mobilize Latinos. First, Latinos are very likely to either be immigrants or to have family members or friends affected by immigration. Studies show that anti-immigrant rhetoric has politically rallied Latinos because anti-immigration policies often manifest themselves as anti-Latino (Barreto 2013). Some studies have also shown that the general experience of discrimination of Latinos has centered around immigration, whether or not the Latino was a U.S. citizen. In other words, Latinos, regardless of their citizenship status, have experienced some type of discrimination based on racial profiling due to immigration concerns (Robert Wood Johnson Foundation 2015). Further, anti-immigrant rhetoric and policy has politically rallied Latinos because both often manifest themselves as anti-Latino. It is important to reiterate that, in a political context, immigration is much more than a talking point; it is personal (Barreto 2013).

The connection between immigration and discrimination may also explain why Latinos with diverse backgrounds—such as Puerto Rican, Cuban, and Colombian—have organized to oppose anti-immigrant policies. For some elected officials, misrepresentation of immigration, which is a popular issue, can easily be promoted without being challenged. For instance, politicians and candidates may disingenuously use pejorative stereotypes when discussing immigrants in order to appeal to their constituent's fears. Therefore, immigrant populations that cannot vote—noncitizens and the undocumented—are subject to further prejudice. It's relatively easy to misrepresent or stereotype Latino immigrants, and, by extension, U.S.-born Latinos, because of a lack of knowledge or widespread misinformation about the community (Santa Ana 2002).

These public officials can also blame—or castigate—immigrants for the economic and social ills in the state, despite the fact that numerous studies have found that immigrants make a positive contribution to the economy (Gans 2008). For instance, public officials have either inflated the actual number of unauthorized immigrants or wrongly blamed them for high crime rates or economic dependency on social welfare programs. For much of the past two decades, the rhetoric on immigration by some prominent leaders has been divisive and hostile (Chávez 2008).

Scholars have also theorized that some of the negative rhetoric by politicians and elected officials targeting Latino immigrants stems from the authoritarian research model. Simply put, forceful authoritarian spokespersons, political candidates, and elected officials can muster support if constituents or voters are frightened of the unknown or unfamiliar. In other words, candidates can generate support because they frighten people into believing that they can protect them from what is terrifying or strange. In 2016, then–Republican presidential candidate Donald Trump blamed immigrants for crime, terrorism, and the failing economy (Gonzales 2017).

A link also exists between related immigration legislation and prevailing economic conditions. For instance, when Arizona's economy was healthy and prosperous, politicians advocated for less restrictive measures for immigrants. There was also aggressive recruitment and outreach for guest workers, especially in the hospitality and construction industries. When the economy collapsed, those efforts fell by the wayside. The economy, either robust or ailing, is one of the most notable influences on immigration legislation. This phenomenon played out nationally in the 1930s during the Great Repatriation, in the 1950s during Operation Wetback, in the 1990s with the passage of Proposition 187, and in the mid–2000s with the Great Recession (Magaña 2014).

Putting the Book into Context

This is the first book that examines Latino politics in Arizona. Arizona Latinos are part of an innovative political strategy called "The Rising American Electorate." This strategy serves to target not only Latinos but other first-time voters. This movement has been very successful in both the 2016 and 2018 elections.[1]

---

1. There have been some excellent studies on Latino politics in other states, such as Benjamin Márquez, *Democratizing Texas Politics: Race, Identity, and Mexican American Empowerment, 1945–2002* (2014), and David R. Ayón and George L. Pla, *Power Shift: How Latinos in California Transformed Politics in America* (2018). In terms of work on mobilization, please see Juan Gómez-Quiñones and Irene Vásquez, *Making Aztlán: Ideology and Culture of the Chicana and Chicano Movement,*

When envisioning this book, we wanted it to be accessible to a general audience while at the same time also useful in the academic setting. We believe this book will make a contribution to the field of Latino politics as well as to sociology, history, American studies, and studies of race and ethnicity, to name but a few.

The origins of this manuscript began approximately ten years ago. In 2010, Arizona passed Senate Bill 1070 (SB 1070), one of the toughest laws that targets unauthorized immigration in the United States. SB 1070 gives police officers in Arizona the latitude to ask anyone about their immigration status. For many, SB 1070 was seen as a way to racially profile Latinos. An academic conference focused on SB 1070 was convened, with experts from various fields, to show how anti-immigration laws like SB 1070 are detrimental not only for Latinos but for the country as a whole. The conference generated many important research findings, as well as an edited book based on the proceedings. Although that volume was published and well received, it still did not capture the broader spirit of Latino politics in Arizona—the topic examined in this book.

This book is based predominately on qualitative methodology. A few interviews, both formal and informal, were conducted over the past ten years with some political players in Arizona. We attended presentations where we were able to have in-depth conversations about the issues with both key and background players that helped shape our understanding of the issue and direction of where Arizona politics is heading. Also, we consulted various

1966–1977 (2014); and Mario T. García, *The Chicano Movement: Perspectives from the Twentieth-First Century* (2014).

For research on immigrants as political activists in other states, see Heather Silber Mohamed, *The New Americans? Immigration, Protest, and the Politics of Latino Identity* (2017); Anna Sampaio, *Terrorizing Latina/o Immigrants: Race, Gender, and Immigration Politics in the Age of Security* (2015); and María Chávez, Jessica L. Lavariega Monforti, and Melissa R. Michelson, *Living the Dream: New Immigration Policies and the Lives of Undocumented Latino Youth* (2015).

In evaluating actual Latino voter turnout, please see Lisa García Bedolla and Melissa R. Michelson, *Mobilizing Inclusion: Transforming the Electorate through Get-Out-the-Vote Campaigns* (2012); Gabriel R. Sánchez, ed., *Latinos and the 2012 Election: The New Face of the American Voter* (2015); Lisa García Bedolla, *Latino Politics* (2014); and John García, *Latino Politics in America* (2016).

secondary sources. We rely heavily on the excellent polling and research data from the Pew Research Center, whose surveys are among the best on Latinos, immigration, and political issues in the United States. We also make use of books, newspaper articles, studies, reports, and archival reports. Overall, we wanted to tell a story about Latino politics in Arizona because it is a new and dynamic topic that is worth learning about, sharing, and emulating.

CHAPTER 1
Latinos in Arizona

The Early Years

Shiree Teng and Tom K. Wong (2016) state that "the current climate for Latinos in Arizona has deep roots." Often lost in the contemporary discussion of immigration and Latino political empowerment in Arizona is the historical fact that a number of Latinos in the state can trace their family roots to pre-Arizona statehood, when Arizona was still part of México. There is a historical, physical, and cultural connection to México that is unique to Arizona (Sheridan 2012). There are Latinos that are newly arrived immigrants, mostly from México, and there are American Latinos that have arrived from other states.

After approximately three hundred years of being colonized, México gained its independence from Spain in 1821 (Ciment and Radzilowski 2014; Sheridan 2012). The Mexican national constitution divided the country into territories and created politically autonomous states. California and New Mexico were territories, while Texas was attached to the larger, more powerful state of Coahuila.

In the 1830s, an expansive proportion of land between México City and its northern territories was uninhabited. México encouraged Americans to make their way into the northern parts of their country by providing them with large, inexpensive tracts of land. A number of American immigrants came from the midwestern, southeastern, and eastern parts of the United States in order to take advantage of the various economic opportunities in Northern México (Anzaldúa 1987)

In 1845, John O'Sullivan, editor of the *New York Morning News*, coined the phrase "manifest destiny." He stated, "It was our manifest destiny to overspread and to possess the whole of the continent which Providence has given us for the development of the great experiment of liberty and federated self-government entrusted to us" (Sheridan 2012). Citizens of the United States believed in the notion that the country had a divine right and an obligation to expand its borders from coast to coast (2012). With this popular rationale, it was natural for American citizens to talk of enlarging their borders and feel that God was on their side. There was a growing sentiment of American superiority and a sense that the nation was divinely guided and supported in their mission to go west and south (2012). On May 13, 1845, Congress overwhelmingly supported going to war with México and gave President Polk approval (Anzaldúa 1987). U.S. troops were sent to the California and New Mexican regions and were met with little resistance when occupying these northern territories; their American inhabitants or immigrants readily accepted the notion of being under the United States' control.

When American troops, under the command of General Winfield Scott, entered México City on September 14, 1847, the Mexican-American War was effectively over. The taking of the Mexican capital and capturing of President Santa Anna delivered a devastating blow to the Mexican people. At the end of the war, the Treaty of Guadalupe Hidalgo was signed on February 2, 1848 (Sheridan 2012). This treaty ceded nearly one-third of its land to the United States, including the Californian and New Mexican territories. The exceptionally vast New Mexican area included parts of modern-day Arizona, Utah, Nevada, and Colorado. Furthermore, México was to relinquish all claims to Texas and agree to recognize the Río Grande as the southern border of the United States.

This new division of México immediately affected nearly three hundred thousand residents, who overnight became citizens of the United States. The signing of the Treaty of Guadalupe-Hidalgo did not complete the annexation; in the years after the Mexican-American War, tensions between the two countries continued to escalate. Both claimed to own the Mesilla Valley, a region now in the state of New Mexico, where the Mexican government evicted American residents. Governor William Lane declared Mesilla Valley part of New Mexico and therefore a part of the United States. Santa Anna escalated the conflict by sending Mexican troops into the valley in order to protect the area for México. President Franklin Pierce sent U.S. minister and railroad speculator James Gadsden to the region in an attempt to strike a compromise (Sheridan 2012).

For Gadsden, the major goal was to purchase land for the creation of the southern transcontinental railroad. President Santa Anna did not want to relinquish any more land but needed money to fund an army in order to put down the various rebellions in México. Gadsden eventually offered $15,000,000 for 45,000 square miles of additional land near the southern part of the United States. When presented with the Gadsden proposal, the Senate reduced the price to $10,000,000. Through the Gadsden Purchase of 1853, the United States gained what became Arizona and New Mexico and created the modern-day southern border of the United States (Sheridan 2012).

After the Gadsden Purchase and the signing of the Treaty of Guadalupe Hidalgo, Mexican Americans in this newly acquired area had little leverage in the negotiation of documents. Anglos quickly migrated to the Southwest in search of land and other economic opportunities in a region with a wealth of untapped resources. As the Anglo presence in the Southwest grew, so did its domination over some of the people of Mexican origin living in the area. It mattered little to some Anglo settlers that the region's previous inhabitants had been here for centuries—or, as was the case for Native Americans, thousands of years. Backed officially by the government, including law enforcement, Anglo settlers began to deny Latinos their property and their civil and social rights as promised by the treaty (Magaña 2014). In 1862, the Homestead Act allowed people to buy land in the Central Valley of Arizona, which contributed to the growth of the Southwest. If the land was occupied for five years and improvements were made, individuals could claim it as their own. Later generations of migrants came predominately from the Midwest.

In the 1870s, laws were passed to limit the rights of Mexican Americans in schooling, housing, public gatherings, and even marriages. As the Anglo population in Arizona grew, Latinos were relegated to a lower sociopolitical status. For instance, a dual wage system for Anglos and Mexican American workers became acceptable practice and was eventually institutionalized (Magaña 2014). Legal discrimination and widening poverty made social advancement increasingly difficult for the vast majority of Mexican Americans and Mexican immigrants. All the while, tensions between these groups and Anglos festered, sometimes erupting into violence (Magaña 2005).

In 1873, Brigham Young, the modern leader of the Mormon church, set up several ministries in the southwest region between Salt Lake City, Utah; Arizona; and a seaport of Guaymas, México (Peterson 1992). By 1878, Arizona missionaries settled in Snowflake, Taylor, St. Johns, Concho, and Eagar. It is important to note that one of the biggest Mormon settlements out of Salt Lake City is in the Mesa, Arizona, region (Peterson 1992). Mesa is the second-largest city in Arizona, and a suburb right outside of Phoenix. Others settled in Pima, Thatcher, and Safford in the Gila River country, and in St. David on the San Pedro River (Peterson 1992). In 1884, David K. Udall and other prominent Mormons in Arizona were imprisoned for practicing plural marriages. In order to flee persecution in the United States, some Mormons fled to México (Peterson 1992).

In 1894, La Alianza Hispana Americana (AHA) was formed in the Arizona-southwestern region by Ramón Soto, Carlos Ignacio Velasco, and Carlos Jácome, among others of Mexican origin (Navarro 2005). This organization provided social activities and low-cost life insurance for its members and focused on politics, civil rights, and education issues after the annexation of México (Noel 2014). These Mexicanos who lived in Tucson provided assistance to Latinos navigating both the new American territory as well as the notion of what it meant to be a U.S. citizen (Noel 2014; Briegel 1974). These immigration assistance organizations called "mutualistas" grew in size and scope throughout the Southwest (Noel 2014; Briegel 1974). In 1897, cofounder Ignacio Calvillo declared it necessary to "protect and fight for the rights of Spanish Americans in Tucson for at that time there was a lot of strife and ill-feeling between us and the Anglo Saxon element that caused in great part by prejudice, misunderstanding and prejudice" (Navarro 2005). Some mutualistas grew into important Latino lobby groups.

As the state expanded, several employment sectors generated a need for Mexican immigrant labor. For instance, the creation of Fort McDowell attracted Sonorans and other Mexican laborers from the surrounding desert region. The agricultural sector was also booming at this time. The Newlands Reclamation Act (1902) allowed Anglo farmers to plant cotton and lettuce on irrigated acreage in the Phoenix and Yuma regions (Magaña 2014).

In the early twentieth century, the industrial metal and mining industry began to flourish, along with the railroad system, throughout the state and country. Also during this period, *Zanjeros* (ditch workers) labored on a system of canals throughout the state that delivered a steady supply of water to valley farmers later known as the Salt River Project. At this time, Mexicans that immigrated or who were recruited to Arizona provided over 13 percent of the territory's population of two hundred thousand in the early 1900s (Magaña 2014).

The Twentieth Century

The period 1910–30 marked an increase in the number of Mexican nationals living in the United States (Powers 2013): in 1900, roughly 100,000 Mexicans, and in the 1930s, nearly 1.5 million. This significant population increase began around the time of the Mexican Revolution, when Mexican citizens left their homeland to seek a better life in the United States. The majority were mestizos (half-Spaniard, half-indigenous). Tired of the persecution they faced, they rebelled in 1910 to gain control over the government and to assert their rights. The revolution resulted in dramatic immigration to the United States. In 1912 alone, 23,328 Mexicans entered the country. Some of these individuals came alone, without spouses or children. Some were professionals such as artists, teachers, and architects who were pursuing political asylum. The four states bordering México on the American side increased substantially in population while the other side in México decreased. At times, entire villages would migrate across the border to be protected from the onslaught of war (Magaña 2014).

On February 14, 1912, Arizona became a state (Vélez-Ibáñez and Szecsy 2014; Santa Ana and González De Bustamante, 2012). More migrants from other parts of the country were settling in Arizona. Opportunities for employment continued to be found in the agricultural, waterway, and mining systems as part of a new growing infrastructure.

Indicative of growing tensions between Latinos and Anglos, in 1916, a strike ensued by the Latino copper miners against the Phelps Dodge Corporation. Latino laborers' pay was almost half that of the Anglo miners. Under the guise of national security, vigilantes in Bisbee, Arizona, asked laborers if they were American citizens; if they were not, they were detained and then transported to México. After the strike was settled, in 1917, the city of Bisbee removed 1,200 Latino laborers. A federal investigation found that the mining companies were at fault. Unfortunately, even with three hundred lawsuits brought on by deportees, only one case actually made it to court, and no legal action resulted. President Woodrow Wilson did not believe the deportations violated any federal laws (Gordon 2001).

Furthermore, schools in Arizona were essentially segregated for Mexican and Mexican American children (Powers 2013). Latino students were directed into English-only Americanization and vocational-skills programs (Vélez-Ibáñez and Szecsy 2014; Powers 2013). Children with Spanish surnames were placed in Americanization programs even if they spoke no Spanish: "Children were punished, spanked, and expelled for speaking Spanish in the schools and in the playgrounds so that generations emerged with a stuttering familiarity with that rich resource and often associated pain with its maintenance as the author's personal experience may verify" (Vélez-Ibáñez & Szecsy 2014).

Carlos Vélez-Ibáñez and Elsie Szecsy (2014) maintain that Mexican American history was denied in schools:

History in fact was and in many ways continues to be taught from either of two approaches: (a) a single historical and cultural prism in which Mexican-origin populations are simply missing from the continent and relegated to be either just another immigrant group, or (b) from a racialized raison d'etre that treats Mexican-origin populations as commodities that engage in back-breaking labor, or persons to be bought and sold, or culturally denigrated without human rights at different and particular points in time. (Vélez-Ibáñez and Szecsy 2014)

In the 1920s and 1930s, the state evolved into a popular destination for vacationing snowbirds: individuals leaving their homes for a temporary stay in Arizona to flee from colder weather. The growing population meant that the state needed more laborers, which led to farmers recruiting Mexican immigrants and setting up stations near the border. In the early 1930s, the overall population of Arizona was approximately four hundred thousand. Sixty thousand were now Latino, half of whom were born in the United States.

In the mid-1930s, one-third of all Americans were unemployed. Popular and political sentiment against the Mexican national emerged. President Herbert Hoover insisted that Mexican immigrants took away American jobs and were responsible for the Depression (Sánchez 1993). Arizona state legislatures enacted laws that made it illegal to hire unauthorized Mexican immigrants, even though they had previously been recruited. Eventually popular sentiment against the Mexican national resulted in mass repatriation or deportation of over one-third of the U.S. Mexican community. Estimates indicate that the total number of deported Mexican nationals and Mexican American citizens was around five hundred thousand (Sánchez 1993).

In the 1940s, the copper, beef, and cotton industries provided materials for wartime goods and services. Furthermore, the desert served as a key location for several military bases and training locations. The population of Arizona continued to grow, almost doubling in size, to approximately eight hundred thousand. The effects of World War II also played a profound role in the development of Mexican American identity and economic prosperity. Servicemen realized that, despite earning the respect of their comrades in arms, they continued to face poor and unequal treatment at home (Sheridan 2012; Ramós 1998). The Servicemen's Readjustment Act—more commonly known as the GI Bill—that President Roosevelt signed into law in 1944 helped improve the lives of many Mexican American veterans and their families (Rosales 2011; Ramós 1998). The legislation gave financial assistance to military veterans to help them readjust to life as civilians. Using these monies, Latinos purchased homes outside of barrios or attended college (Rosales 2011).

The rapidly expanding post–World War II economy produced a substantial manpower shortage in the United States. To meet it, the United States and México instituted a contracted worker system called the Bracero Program in 1942 (Sheridan 2012; Ramós 1998). This initiative allowed agricultural employers in the United States to recruit and hire low-cost Mexican laborers, who were granted temporary worker status, on a seasonal basis. Unfortunately, employers had wide discretion over pay, as well as working and living conditions for the immigrant workers (Ramós 1998). Critics have described the Bracero Program as a virtual slave labor system because of its legacy of widespread worker and human rights abuses. As a result of the substandard labor conditions often endured by the Braceros, in Arizona some immigrants sidestepped the program and entered the country illegally (Ramós 1998; Navarro 2005).

The strong U.S. economy during this period further fueled the growth of the Mexican American community. An estimated four million workers came to the United States from México, with more than 90 percent working in the states of Arizona, California, New Mexico, and Texas (Bittersweet 2010; Navarro 2005). Also fueling Arizona's population growth were servicemen stationed in the state during World War II who were now returning home. In the late 1940s, thousands migrated to Arizona. Estimates of the population grew to around one million. After the war, the state continued to boom, attracting a large number of high-tech, engineering, and manufacturing companies.

Perhaps not so surprising, but one of the most important factors that led to migration from other states, was the invention of the air conditioner. From all accounts, it was this device that essentially opened up Arizona to mass migration from all over the country. The state also relied more heavily on the tourism sector: several luxurious vacation resorts were built during this period using Mexican immigrant labor. The state remains a popular destination for individuals from other states with colder climates.

An economic recession in the early 1950s again turned popular sentiment against Mexican immigrants. As a result, the Immigration and Naturalization Service (INS) began expelling Mexican nationals, some of them in the country legally, through a program known as "Operation Wetback," beginning in 1954. According to the INS, apprehensions and deportations reached 1,300,000 that year. During the next five years, the INS deported approximately 3.8 million Mexican nationals (Magaña 2014).

As a result of the U.S. economy's diversification in the 1950s, a growing number of unauthorized immigrants looked for higher-paying, urban-based jobs in the manufacturing and industrial sectors. It was during this period that the Mexican American population began its shift from residing in rural areas to the urban communities where they are predominately located today. Enticed by a growing economy and inexpensive housing, Latinos migrated to Arizona.

Latinos in both rural and urban areas continued to be discriminated against in the state. Some restaurants, businesses, churches, and theaters persisted in segregating Mexican Americans (Powers 2013). Property covenants prohibited Mexican Americans from purchasing or renting property in certain communities (Sheridan 2012; Powers 2013). The Phoenix Real Estate Board blocked realtors from "introducing into a neighborhood of any race or nationality, or any individuals detrimental to property values in that neighborhood" (Vélez-Ibáñez and Szecsy 2014).

Besides the overt oppression in schools, work sites, and public spaces, schemes focused on the restructuring of voting further politically alienated Latinos in Phoenix (Vélez-Ibáñez and Szecsy 2014). In the late 1950s, the city of Phoenix changed its voting scheme from a district-voting to an at-large voting scheme (Sheridan 2012). In an at-large voting scheme, the candidate that gets the most votes wins; in a district-voting scheme, only those individuals that live in the district can run for election, and only those from the same district can vote for the candidate. The result is that, in a district voting scheme, a candidate can run an election at a lower cost. It also ensures that the candidate will fairly represent the district that they are from. In short,

> Mexicans in general lost whatever political influence they had in the 1920s by the restructuring of Phoenix government into new wards in which each elected their own city councilmen in the 1960s. Wards 1 and 2 were dominated by Anglos, and 3 and 4 were located in south Phoenix where most Mexicans and African Americans lived except that the new city commission members in any Ward were to be elected at large. This resulted in the disenfranchisement of those in wards 3 and 4 since the demographics were against them. (Vélez-Ibáñez and Szecsy 2014)

The 1960s was a time of civil reform during which the passage of laws like the Voting Rights Act encouraged greater political participation by African Americans and Latinos. In 1965, a major immigration act led to a major demographic shift, allowing Latino American immigrants that had been barred entry to the United States to be admitted. Simply put, Asians, Africans, and Latin Americans began entering the United States in significant numbers, dramatically changing the makeup of the country.

The Chicano Movement

The 1960s also marked the birth of the Chicano Movement, also known as *El Movimiento* (The movement): a "heterogeneous political reform movement comprised of 'multiple' leaders, organizations, competing ideologies, and protest mobilization strategies and tactics" that was partly revolutionist but essentially reformist in nature and wholeheartedly committed to fundamental social change (Navarro 2005). The movement helped spawn hundreds of organizations nationwide, including the United Farm Workers Union, La Raza Unida Party, La Alianza de Pueblos Libres, the Brown Berets, the National Chicano Moratorium, the Crusade for Justice, the Mexican American Youth Organization, and Movimiento Estudiantil Chicano de Aztlán (MEChA; Rosales 1997).

El Movimiento championed several major objectives— defending labor rights (especially for nonunionized farmworkers); ending segregation, discrimination, political repression, and land grant struggles in border states; demanding increased educational opportunities in public schools, colleges, and universities; and "[seeking] political empowerment and inclusion for Mexican Americans and Chicanos and Chicanas" (Santa Ana and González De Bustamante 2012).

El Movimiento began with a strike/boycott by the United Farm Workers (UFW) union on grape growers in California on September 16, 1965. Interestingly, the movement became divided over the issue of immigration. Labor activist César Chávez excluded undocumented laborers from the movement because of potential negative negotiations; he felt that these workers made the struggle for "legal" recognition more difficult (Rosales 1997).

El Movimiento was "particularly strong among Chicano and Chicana students at the college level . . . who formed organizations and advocated for educational reforms and Chicano Studies curricula" (Santa Ana and González De Bustamante 2012). Universities would become its intellectual and spiritual stronghold. By the 1960s, Mexican Americans had begun to reap the rewards of educational advancement also made possible by the GI Bill. This meant that a growing number of Latinos acquired higher degrees. Chicano studies and other Latino programs nationwide became part of the legacy of that movement.

El Movimiento Estudiantil Chicano de Aztlán (MEChA) also sprang from the Chicano Movement—or El Movimiento—and still operates today. The organization, Lee Bebout (2016) explains, "formed at the height of the Chicano movement MEChA is known for its efforts to foster Chicano consciousness and grow Chicano influence in educational institutions" (99). MEChA has over four hundred affiliate chapters in schools and universities, mainly in the southwest, that encourage political empowerment for Latino youth.

In 1969, community and student activists in Arizona founded Chicanos Por La Causa (CPLC) "to address the problems of the barrios of South-Central Phoenix" (CPLC Nevada n.d.). Initially, the CPLC aimed to create jobs and improve the quality of life in the Chicano community. However, CPLC found that the community had many other issues that also needed to be addressed. Since the 1960s, the organization has dramatically expanded, providing services in both urban and rural areas. Outreach is both bilingual and bicultural in Arizona, New Mexico, and Nevada and assists two hundred thousand low-income people yearly throughout the Southwest (n.d.). Although originally created to help Chicanos in Central Phoenix, the CPLC maintains that the organization "develops programs and services that address these needs, regardless of ethnicity, gender, age, or creed" (n.d.).

One notable activist to come out of the Chicano movement in Arizona is Alfredo Gutiérrez. Born and raised in Miami, Arizona, Gutiérrez enlisted in the army and enrolled at Arizona State University (ASU) using the GI Bill. He led a student strike against the administration because of the treatment of laundry workers at the university. When he left ASU, he was an organizer for the United Farm Workers and one of the founders of CPLC. He also organized in the Phoenix Union High School District and Maricopa County for the adoption of better access to Medicaid in Arizona. Gutiérrez ran for the Arizona Senate as a Democrat in 1972 and was elected majority leader in 1974. For fourteen years thereafter, he served as either majority or minority leader. He maintains that "along with Burton Barr, Art Hamilton, and Governor Bruce Babbitt, led the reorganization of State government from a rural, southern-inspired governance model to a modern, forward-leaning decision structure" (Maricopa Community Colleges 2016).

In the mid-1970s, Latino unauthorized immigration continued to rise, fueled by an ailing Mexican economy as well as their need for employment. The state's economy saw significant growth during this period, due in part to a heavy reliance on cheap labor, specifically for the housing-construction and tourism industries. These two sectors helped Arizona to develop some of the most luxurious resorts in the country, which boosts the state's economy due to the many retirees who chose to live their golden years in Arizona and call it home.

During the 1970s, Raul Hector Castro, another Latino activist, gained popular and political prominence in the state. Born in Cananea, Sonora, México, Castro moved with his family in 1920 to Pirtleville, Arizona, a mining town near Douglas. Castro would recount how, while working as a miner, the showers in the mines were segregated for white and Mexican workers, and that the public pool at the local YMCA could only be used by Mexicans on a day that it would be cleaned. These formative experiences shaped and influenced his political career. After graduating from high school, he secured an athletic scholarship to the Arizona State Teachers College (now known as Northern Arizona University). During one summer between semesters, he returned home and worked in the smelters' mine to help pay for school. Noticing that there was no labor union, he rallied his coworkers, later persuading a professional union organizer from Jerome to help establish the first union for smelter laborers—the Mine Mill Smelter Workers of America—and, a year or so later, in 1937, to secure a contract with Phelps Dodge.

By 1939, Castro graduated from the Arizona State Teachers College with a bachelor of arts degree. Finding a teaching job proved impossible, because discrimination against Mexican Americans kept them from being hired. He did, however, have success with boxing and laboring in agricultural fields. After returning to Douglas, he was eventually hired at the American consulate in nearby Agua Prieta, Sonora, México, for the U.S. State Department. For five years he worked on diplomatic issues between México and the United States. He eventually moved to Tucson and found a job teaching Spanish while he attended the University of Arizona School of Law, from which he graduated in 1949. He was elected a Pima County attorney and then Pima County superior court judge. Castro then became ambassador to El Salvador, confirmed by president Lyndon B. Johnson. In the 1970s, he played a pivotal role in arranging a meeting between the presidents of the five Central American countries and was later appointed ambassador to Bolivia.

In 1970, Raul Hector Castro announced his campaign for governor of Arizona. He ran on a platform of pollution control, drug abuse prevention, and the improvement of business and cultural relations with México. He won the democratic primary but lost the gubernatorial race to the incumbent governor by a narrow margin of 1.8 percent. He ran again in 1974, this time gaining support from many Native Americans. That year Castro became the first and only Latino governor of Arizona (Santa Ana and González De Bustamante 2012). Two years into his position as governor, he accepted president Jimmy Carter's offer to serve as ambassador to Argentina. In 1980, he stepped down as ambassador and returned to Phoenix to practice law. He died in 2015 at the age of ninety-eight.

Contemporary Immigration

In 1986, the U.S. Congress passed the Immigration Reform and Control Act (IRCA). IRCA's overall objective was to decrease the number of unauthorized immigrants in the United States by implementing two provisions: employer sanctions and a legalization process (Santa Ana and González De Bustamante 2012). The employer sanctions provisions were designed to deter immigrants seeking employment in the United States. IRCA mandated that legal employees must show proof or documentation when applying for employment, and that employers who do not comply with IRCA would be sanctioned. The law is still intact.

The legalization provision, also known as "amnesty," meant to legalize the status of unauthorized immigrants already in the United States, thus reducing the total number of unauthorized individuals residing within the country (Santa Ana and González De Bustamante 2012). It was a one-time-only policy: only immigrants that had entered the country prior to 1982 and resided in the country continually for four years could apply. Overall, IRCA resulted in the processing of almost three million immigrants seeking legalized status. In addition, seven million employers had to be trained on the objectives of employer sanctions provisions. In 1986, IRCA was the first and only comprehensive immigration that addressed both the enforcement and service aspects of immigration. Policy makers have tried to pass some sort of comprehensive immigration since the 1980s but have been unsuccessful.

It is important to note that the policy was passed during a Republican administration. Since then, there has been a discernible shift in the Republican attitude toward immigration. It is fair to maintain that the Democratic and Republican parties are fairly distinct in their stance on immigration. Furthermore, the amnesty provision has been met with criticism. Some critics maintain that the policy only served as an incentive for more immigrants to enter illegally, and that they are never punished for unlawful entry. Interestingly, recent debates regarding immigration have centered on supporters of "amnesty-type" immigration proposals. That is, some politicians do not want to look soft on immigration and will criticize those that do or have supported legalization proposals.

When Congress passed IRCA, the Immigration and Naturalization Service (INS) was responsible for its implementation. Some of the main INS players would later go on to create an organization called the Federation for American Immigration Reform (FAIR), which became responsible for many of the anti-immigrant proposals in Arizona and across the country (Lacayo 2011).

In 1990, federal immigration policy was again overhauled, in order to address authorized and unauthorized immigration. Under the Immigration Act of 1990, the number of immigrants under the "flexible cap" grew to 675,000, and funding for more Border Patrol operations was increased to allow the hiring of 1,000 more agents. Additionally, agency guidelines were rewritten regarding the exclusion, naturalization, and deportation of unauthorized immigrants. For one, the act allowed the attorney general to grant temporary protected status to undocumented alien nationals of designated countries subject to armed conflict or natural disasters. Also in the 1990s, unauthorized immigration became a target of popular reform, particularly in states like California, Texas, and Florida, where immigrant communities flourished. These states falsely blamed immigrants for their strained public resources and sued the federal government for reimbursement costs, maintaining that it had failed to fulfill its responsibility to control immigration. In 1994, during the Clinton administration, Arizona demanded $121 million to cover the costs incurred by unauthorized immigrants in the state's prison system.

In California, after federal cutbacks and the loss of approximately half a million defense-related jobs, the state's economy was in crisis, and the unemployment rate had jumped to 8.6 percent, about two percentage points higher than the national average. Conservative leaders in California attributed the state's problems to the presence of unauthorized immigrants. Governor Pete Wilson capitalized on this sentiment during his bid for reelection by championing Proposition 187, a 1994 ballot initiative that would have prohibited unauthorized immigrants from using health care, public education, and other social services statewide (Rodríguez and Rouse 2012; Pantoja et al. 2001). In November 1994, voters passed the law and reelected Wilson. Governor Wilson tried to use his success in California to mount a presidential bid, but he failed to gain momentum.

Proposition 187, known as the "Save Our State Initiative," intended to force school districts and postsecondary institutions to stop providing educational services to unauthorized students. School administrators would be required to verify the immigration status of all newly admitted students as well as the status of their parents. Students and parents unable to verify their status were to be reported to the U.S. Immigration and Naturalization Service (now part of the Department of Homeland Security) and the California attorney general. This initiative also prohibited all hospital administrators, both public and private, from providing nonemergency healthcare to unauthorized immigrants.

The courts have ruled in the past (e.g., *Plyler v. Doe*, 1982) that children, regardless of their status, can attend grammar school, high school, and college. Furthermore, everyone can receive emergency services, regardless of their status. Proposition 187 was ultimately found to be unconstitutional when the courts ruled that only the federal government, not a state, can pass and implement immigration laws. Proposition 187 is important because it set the political agenda of limiting welfare to discourage unauthorized immigration, even though unauthorized immigrants cannot use welfare. Proposition 187 also set into motion a political movement for states to increase pressure on federal authorities to address undocumented immigration.

The North American Free Trade Agreement (NAFTA) between the United States, México, and Canada further affected immigration to Arizona. Signed on January 1, 1992, NAFTA removed most trade barriers between the three countries in order to encourage trade. In short, after NAFTA, the rich got richer, and the poor got poorer. One example of NAFTA's devastating effects can be seen in corn farming. Post-NAFTA, the prices paid to Mexican farmers for the production of corn plummeted by 66 percent, forcing many out of business altogether. This drop-in payment resulted in many Mexican farmers losing their lands and going into debt that most could not pay. This created an unworkable economic system where Mexicans were no longer able to live off of the land and were forced to look for other alternatives to make ends meet, such as crossing into the United States illegally to work in the higher-paying agricultural industry. The trade agreement removed tariffs on corn while also eliminating subsidizes for small farmers. NAFTA, however, allowed for U.S. subsidies, making it nearly impossible for small farms to continue producing corn.

Furthermore, the monetary unit of México, the peso, experienced periods of devaluation that rocked the Mexican economy and spurred further immigration into the United States. In 1994, the collapse of the peso, known popularly as the "Tequila Crisis," resulted in the peso amounting to almost a 50-percent drop in value in six months (Magaña 2014). One cause of the crisis was the massive increase in spending by president Carlos Salinas de Gortari, causing México to increase its foreign debt substantially. The political turmoil that accompanied this election cycle, capped off by the assassination of Luis Donaldo Colosio, discouraged investors from placing their money into the Mexican economy. Left without homes, businesses, and the ability to make a decent income, many Mexicans sought to live in the United States.

Furthermore, the wages of Mexican workers in the United States in comparison to wages in México were high and influenced immigration into the United States. This increase in Mexican laborers coming to the United States continued until the late 2000s. Another push factor, prevalent in recent years, is the drug trade in México, which has been embroiled in a drug war, causing significant destruction throughout the country, particularly in border areas between the United States and México. As of 2013, it is estimated that nearly forty thousand people have died in this war on drugs.

Most important, federal enforcement border policies were implemented in 1994–95 that essentially redirected immigration from California and Texas into Arizona (Santa Ana and González De Bustamante 2012). "Operation Gatekeeper" in California and "Operation Hold-the-Line" in Texas decreased unauthorized entries by boosting the number of federal agents assigned to the regions around Tijuana/San Diego and Ciudad Juárez/El Paso. Hundreds of millions of dollars flowed into the budget to increase the number of agents patrolling high-volume crossing points. These policies redirected immigration into Arizona into substantially less populated and more tortuous Sonoran-Arizona desert (Santa Ana and González De Bustamante 2012). As a result, anti-immigration initiatives started to grow in Arizona in the mid-1990s.

It is imperative to note that, while immigration increased in Arizona, the overall state economy was booming. During the 1990s, Arizona was one of the top seven states in the country that experienced the most economic success. Major high-tech companies, such as Intel, resettled in the state. Investments from other states were also made in major shopping and retail developments. Several large casinos were also built in Arizona.

Property was relatively inexpensive in Phoenix. With the growth of employment opportunities and the ability to purchase property in Arizona, the state experienced another population boom. Overall, by the late 1990s, Arizona's population was being fueled by (mostly Mexican) immigration, as well as the migration of nonimmigrant individuals from other states. The state also continued to attract older residents who wished to retire there.

CHAPTER 2

The Building Blocks of Change

The debate over states' rights versus what some contend is too much federalism is alive and well in Arizona. For most of the past fifteen years, a number of key policy players argued that the state needed more authority to formulate and implement immigration law. These Arizona leaders contend that the federal government is out of touch and overbearing when it comes to finding the best solution for immigration reform. This chapter examines the chain of legislative actions in Arizona that led to the passage of increasingly punitive immigration laws.

Additionally, this chapter documents how key policy players, mainly politicians, introduced immigration initiatives to appeal to its loyal base of constituents in order to advance an anti-immigrant agenda. Although several of these initiatives were hastily formulated and largely symbolic, they were nevertheless politically popular. This chapter also shows how these politicians were motivated and supported by an anti-immigrant base.

Anti-Immigration Starts Growing in Arizona

In 1996, Congress passed the Personal Responsibility and Work Opportunity Reconciliation Act—or the Welfare Act—as a measure to target both "legal" and "illegal" immigrants, aiming to restrict their welfare benefits. Of great importance was that this legislation now denied current "legal" immigrants from receiving a wide range of social services including food stamps and social security until they became citizens (Ciment and Radzilowski 2014). Prior to this act, lawful permanent residents were generally eligible for assistance, similar to U.S. citizens. Some of these immigrants were senior citizens who, under the Welfare Act, would no longer be eligible for social security benefits. This particular provision was very unpopular, and Congress eventually rescinded the policy, with President Clinton vetoing the reform (Parrott et al. 1998).

Unauthorized immigrants cannot technically receive social services such as welfare. Yet, during the mid-to-late 1990s, some politicians, in an effort to make a case for welfare reform and anti-immigration legislation, maintained that immigrants come to this country for welfare benefits or food subsidies, when this has not in fact been the case. Although, assuredly, there are cases where unauthorized immigrants have fraudulently received benefits, studies consistently show that the number-one reason immigrants come to the United States is for employment, not welfare (Anti-Defamation League n.d.).

Legislation to Intimidate Immigrants

Further building on growing anti-immigrant sentiment, in 1996 Congress increased criminal penalties for immigration-related offenses. When the federal Illegal Immigration Reform and Immigrant Responsibility Act (IIRIRA) was passed, a largely unnoticed provision—287(g)—authorized state and local police officers to collaborate with the federal government to carry out immigration policies. After the 2003 formation of the U.S. Immigration and Customs Enforcement (ICE), local police worked in tandem with the agency to perform limited immigration law enforcement functions (US Immigration and Customs Enforcement 2020). The 287(g) provision, still in effect nationwide, authorizes the secretary of the U.S. Department of Homeland Security to work with local law enforcement agencies, which allows federally trained officers to implement immigration policies. Officers must receive some training from ICE instructors. The stated goal of this coordinated effort is to give local police the necessary resources and latitude to pursue investigations relating to immigrant-related violent crimes, human smuggling, gang/organized crime activity, sexual-related offenses, narcotics smuggling, and money laundering (Department of Homeland Security 2009). Critics of the policy have long argued that 287(g) would lead to civil rights abuses. Arizona's immigrants' rights advocates have documented multiple instances in which local authorities have overstepped their boundaries.

In Chandler, Arizona, in 1997, local authorities partnered with federal agents to implement "Operation Restoration." Presumably, the idea was to "restore" the community to a time when immigrants did not exist. Chandler police officers launched a dragnet to detain people whom they believed to be immigrants, demanding that they prove their citizenship. If the person failed to provide purportedly proper documentation, or if local authorities simply believed the documentation provided was not valid, the suspected immigrants were threatened with deportation or removal. More than four hundred people were detained as part of Operation Restoration, including many Latinos who were U.S. citizens.

The City of Chandler was sued and ultimately required to pay fines as part of court settlements. The U.S. Justice Department ruled that the Chandler police acted improperly and were not adequately trained. The city has not pursued similar enforcement activities since Operation Restoration and has spent the past fifteen years restoring its own reputation by establishing a wide range of racially inclusive policies designed to make amends for its behavior in 1997.

Death at the Border

In the wake of U.S. Border Patrol crackdowns in Texas and California, human rights groups began to document an alarming increase in the number of immigrant deaths in the Arizona desert that virtually quadrupled between 1993 and 1999, after the passage of "Operation Gatekeeper" (California) and "Operation Hold the Line" (Texas).

Temperatures in the largely barren desert in and around the Arizona-México border can reach a staggering 120 degrees. Many immigrants attempting to cross through the region simply die of thirst. The number found dead continues to escalate every year. In response, human rights groups such as No More Deaths, have established makeshift water stations, a practice that generated national controversy from critics who claimed the water stations made crossing the desert more attractive. Although activists in Arizona were arrested and sentenced to jail under littering violations, No More Deaths activists vowed that they would continue their work, claiming that no one should be denied water and die for trying to seek a better life.

The Consequences of 9/11

The attacks on the World Trade Center and the Pentagon on September 11, 2001, prompted a new wave of immigration policy mandates. Immediately afterward, the U.S. Border Patrol was ordered to seal off the nation's southern border and deploy agents to airports. Because of the horrific death toll and the fact that several of the terrorists had legally entered the country with visas, general public sentiment against immigrants grew and expanded from unauthorized immigration across our borders to immigrants overall, particularly those known as "visa overstayers": people who had remained in the United States beyond the time allotted by the federal government, including tourists, international students, and so-called temporary workers. Politicians, quick to respond to popular sentiment, pursued a variety of new immigration-related initiatives to stem visa overstays and prevent terrorism.

In its effort to stop terrorism, the U.S. government formulated a new system for reporting the status of foreign and exchange students. Congress also disbanded the Immigration and Naturalization Service (INS). The agency's two functions, enforcement and immigration services, were separated and placed under the supervision of the newly formed Department of Homeland Security. Border Patrol activities were assigned to the Bureau of Customs and Border Protection, while the previous immigration services of the INS became part of the Bureau of Citizenship and Immigration Services. The agency's previous responsibilities for regulating immigration shifted, bolstering a new emphasis on national security and the deterrence of terrorism. The new mandate increased scrutiny of foreign visitors; although none of the terrorists involved in the 9/11 attacks crossed the Southwest border, legally or otherwise, conservative Republicans in Arizona and elsewhere seized the opportunity to highlight the potential dangers of unauthorized cross-border immigration.

Making matters worse, fear and concern over terrorism and immigration was exacerbated when it turned out that several of the 9/11 terrorists had lived briefly in the Phoenix area. Some people believed that metropolitan Phoenix was home to a "sleeper cell" in support of 9/11 mastermind Osama bin Laden (Wagner and Zoellner 2001). Notably, Lotfi Raissi lived in North Phoenix and provided flight training to four of the terrorists in Arizona. Hani Hanjoor and Nawaf Al-Hazmi, two of the terrorists on the commercial flight that intentionally crashed into the Pentagon, had lived in Phoenix and took flight-training courses in Arizona. As a result, rumors ran rampant that terrorists planned to enter the United States by crossing through the southern border, and anti-Muslim hysteria spread. Tragically, four days after 9/11, a man from Mesa, Arizona, was charged with murder after slaying a bearded, turban-wearing Sikh of Indian origin, whom the killer had mistaken for an Arab Muslim (Magaña 2014).

Prior to 9/11, President Bush had announced that he was considering the creation of a new comprehensive immigration policy. He also talked about better relations with México. In fact, after his second inauguration, his first state dinner was with Vicente Fox, president at the time of México. After national security concerns became a priority for the country due to 9/11, some members of the Republican Party scapegoated Mexican immigrants and blamed them for terrorism as well. Interestingly, when the Department of Homeland Security (DHS) was created, immigration enforcement was drastically restructured on the southern border.

The Canadian and U.S. border is significantly larger than the border between the United States and México. Furthermore, real, documented threats of terrorism or national security have occurred on the Canadian border, not the Mexican border. Yet, significantly more border patrol and enforcement activities took place on the Mexican border under the guise of national security after 9/11.

Anti-Immigrant Vigilante Groups

In 2002, anti-immigrant vigilante groups gained popularity, most notably Civil Homeland Defense and the Minuteman Project. Volunteers from across the country came to Arizona to help patrol and seal the border, using everything from binoculars to high-tech surveillance equipment. Minutemen members cannot legally engage in contact with unauthorized immigrants, but can only report their whereabouts, although several members have been arrested on illegal weapons charges and the unauthorized detention of immigrants. Civil rights organizations such as the Southern Poverty Law Center have documented affiliations between the Minuteman Project and Civil Homeland Defense with neo-Nazi and Aryan Nation organizations, among other white supremacist organizations.

Costs and Benefits of Immigration in Arizona

In 2003, Arizona became the busiest crossing point for immigrants in the nation, while Arizona's foreign-born population grew. In the 1990s, about 268,700 foreign-born persons resided in the state, making up approximately 7.3 percent of the total population. By 2004, the number of foreign-born residents increased over 200 percent to 830,900 persons, doubling their portion of the total population, and making up 14.5 percent (Gans 2008).

Judith Gans (2008), from the University of Arizona, used the available data from 2004 to analyze the "economic consequences of immigrants (from all nations) in Arizona" (p. V). Her study took into account taxes as well as the costs of education, health care, and law enforcement. In her study, Gans (2008) found that

> the total state tax revenue attributable to immigrant workers was an estimated $2.4 billion (about $860 million for naturalized citizens plus about $1.5 billion for non-citizens). Balanced against incremental fiscal costs of $1.4 billion for immigrants in Arizona generated a net 2004 fiscal contribution of about $940 million toward services such as public safety, libraries, road maintenance, and other areas. . . . The 2004 total economic output attributable to immigrant workers was about $44 billion ($15 billion for naturalized citizens and $29 billion for non-citizens). This output included $20 billion in labor and other income and resulted in approximately 400,000 full-time-equivalent jobs.

This study is significant for several reasons. Gans (2008) found that immigrants in Arizona overwhelmingly contribute to the economy, and that unauthorized immigrants contribute more than legal immigrants. The number of immigrants in Arizona was historically high in 2004, and yet their presence is still an overall net gain for the state's economy. These economic facts are not widely publicized or known. In fact, some elected officials have criticized the presence of immigrants and maintained that they are a drain on the economy.

Increasing Anti-immigrant Legislation

In 2004, a group called Protect Arizona Now (PAN) collected enough signatures to place Proposition 200—the Arizona Taxpayer Citizen Protection Act—on the ballot. The policy was formulated to block unauthorized immigrants from receiving government-funded services in Arizona and voting, even though unauthorized immigrants cannot vote or receive welfare or social services in Arizona.

Supporters of the act believed, inaccurately, that immigrants were coming to Arizona to vote illegally. Part of Proposition 200 ensured that immigrant voter fraud would be deterred by placing more restrictions on the types of identification that can be shown in order to vote. For instance, a voter in Arizona must show proof of U.S. citizenship when registering to vote or voting at polling places; voter registration cards would no longer be accepted. In Arizona, you also have to be a citizen to get a driver's license. For some individuals that did not have a birth certificate, passport, or license, this policy essentially excluded them from voting.

Furthermore, Proposition 200 directed officials to review proof of status when immigrants applied for state public welfare benefits, although unauthorized immigrants are excluded from receiving any welfare. The policy also mandated that government workers alert immigration officials of suspected unauthorized immigrants seeking benefits (Avalos et al. 2010). PAN received substantial financial support from some of the vigilante border patrol groups and national anti-immigrant organizations, such as Federation for American Immigration Reform (FAIR) and Americans for Better Immigration. The goals of these and other right-wing groups included increased federal law enforcement on the border (which critics classify as "militarization"), major decreases or a moratorium on legal immigration, the mass deportation of unauthorized immigrants, and concerted opposition to so-called "amnesty" proposals or immigrant guest-worker programs.

Resistance to Proposition 200 came from a broad-based coalition of bipartisan political leaders and organizations representing business, labor, health care, the Latino community, and various religious denominations who formed the No on 200 or Arizonans for Real Immigration Reform (ARIR) committee. Former Arizona attorney general Grants Woods, a Republican, chaired the committee group and received major financial backing from the pro-immigrant and politically liberal Service Employees International Union (Avalos et al. 2010).

Joining the opposition to Proposition 200 were Democratic governor Janet Napolitano and Republican senator John McCain, as well as organizations such as the Republican-led (though officially nonpartisan) Arizona Chamber of Commerce, the Arizona Civil Liberties Union of Arizona, AFL-CIO Arizona, the Arizona Democratic Party, and the Arizona Education Association. 2004 marked an inflection point of public bi-partisan opposition to anti-immigration legislation in Arizona. 56 percent of Arizonans voted yes on Proposition 200. Support for the initiative was highest among white Republican voters and lowest among Latino Democrats. 2004 was also a threshold in a widening political chasm between Arizona Latinos and the state's Republican leadership.

It should be noted that any burdens or obstacles that limit an individual's ability to participate in politics are challenged under the Voting Rights Act. Organizations such as the Mexican American Legal Defense and Educational Fund (MALDEF) and the American Civil Liberties Union (ACLU) have opposed Proposition 200 because of the undue burden it has placed on voters to provide adequate documentation. For instance, senior citizens and Native Americans have challenged the law because they may not be able to provide the required documentation and therefore cannot vote.

More Anti-Immigrant Legislation

In the years after 2004, several policies were passed in Arizona that targeted unauthorized immigration. Again, the United States Constitution stipulates that only the federal government can create and implement immigration laws. The courts have also ruled that children, regardless of their legal status, can attend school. Furthermore, everyone can receive emergency medical services, regardless of their status. To elude this stipulation of the Constitution, in 2004, Arizona focused on "issues related to" immigration which could not be challenged, rather than immigration laws that could be challenged on the basis of the state attempting to control immigration or making its own immigration laws. In 2006, voter-approved initiatives were passed that further illustrated the growing anti-immigrant—especially anti-Latino immigrant—sentiment in Arizona: for example, a proposition that all governmental materials be provided in English only. Despite the fact that the Voting Rights Act dictates that governmental material must be provided in languages other than English if there is an immigrant population, this law was passed.

Arizonans also approved Proposition 100, 102, and 300 in 2006. Proposition 100 denied bail for unauthorized immigrants. Proposition 102 prohibited an unauthorized immigrant from bringing a lawsuit to court or winning damages. For instance, if an immigrant is hurt at a worksite because of employer negligence, they cannot claim damages.

Shutting Down Dreams of Higher Education

One of the more draconian policies passed in 2006 was Proposition 300, which made any unauthorized immigrant immediately ineligible for in-state college tuition, government grants, scholarships, or financial aid. After the passage of this proposition, students who were born in México but had lived in Arizona the majority of their life, and whose parents may or may not have paid state sales taxes and income taxes for years, were charged out-of-state tuition. At community colleges and universities across Arizona, immigrant students dropped their courses because they could not afford the tripling of their tuition and the ban on their receiving scholarships.

Criminalizing the Day Laborer

Even as the state's housing and tourism industries boomed, resentment over immigrant day laborers (many of whom were undocumented) escalated in Phoenix. Other cities across the country grappled with the day labor issues as well. Some immigrant advocates say that cities should provide locations for workers to congregate, while critics maintain that day labor sites encourage unauthorized immigration and flaunt the breaking of federal law. Approximately two dozen business owners in Central Phoenix hired off-duty police officers to remove day laborers from their property. In response, immigrant advocates called for the boycott of these businesses.

Also, in 2006, buckling to public pressure to to address immigration, Governor Napolitano (Democrat) signed House Bill 2592 into law, which prohibited cities in Arizona from funding day labor sites. Due to the fact that funding generally came from private organizations not affiliated with the state government, day labor sites began to shut down as the economy began to slide into recession and private donations dwindled. Further, legislation would soon follow that would make it illegal for anyone to stop or delay traffic to pick up a day laborer for hire.

The Fight for the Border Wall

In 2005, the House of Representatives passed the Border Protection, Anti-Terrorism, and Illegal Immigration Control Act of 2005 (H.R. 4437), also known as the Sensenbrenner Immigration Bill. This legislation charged unauthorized immigrants with a felony, criminalizing what had previously been a purely civil offense. This was especially punitive, because if an immigrant is charged with a felony, they can never gain naturalized status or become a U.S. citizen. One year later, Congress then enacted the Secure Fence Act of 2006. With this act, the DHS intended to secure approximately seven hundred miles of the two-thousand-mile border between the United States and México. Using an allocated $1.2 billion, DHS was charged with overseeing the construction of a triple-layered fence that proponents claimed would be impenetrable by unauthorized immigrants. Federal monies were also provided for more surveillance cameras, motion sensors, and the strengthening of existing barriers.

Republican Senator McCain, and then Democratic Senators Obama and Clinton all supported the wall. The policy failed to meet expectations; only a portion of the wall was ever completed, and only a very small section of the wall is actually triple layered. Federal officials said the fence project failed because of escalating costs and engineering problems.

In Arizona, a wall made of a triple-layered fence was never feasible, due to the region's geography. Areas along Arizona's border are mountainous, while the fence concept would work most effectively on flat terrain. Furthermore, Native American families on the Tohono O'odham Indian Reservation complained that the barrier built on their land desecrates ancient burial sites, and that the extra patrols disrupt the tribe's daily life (Wood 2008). Environmentalists also say that the wall obstructs the natural migration of wildlife, including some endangered species.

Besides the obvious environmental issues, as well as the fact that a wall is spatially impossible and expensive to build, it is imperative to note that almost half of the unauthorized immigration population is made up of visa overstayers. These immigrants that entered the United States legally, with visas; however, they did not leave the country when the visa expired. This means that a wall neither addressed nor deterred nearly half of an estimated eleven to twelve million unauthorized immigrants.

In response to these laws, immigrant rights' groups nationwide organized mass protests involving hundreds of thousands of people. 2006 was the year that the pro-immigration movement really developed nationally. For instance, in Arizona, Latino grassroots organizations orchestrated some of the largest street protests in the state's history. On March 24, 2006, more than 20,000 protesters, mostly Latinos, gathered in downtown Phoenix, marching and chanting "Somos America," or "We are America." The protestors called for an end to anti-immigrant legislation and for support for a national comprehensive immigration reforms that would legalize the millions of undocumented immigrants living in the country. The demonstration made national headlines. The following month, on April 10, 2006, an estimated 125,000 to 200,000 people trekked two-and-a-half miles from the Arizona Fairgrounds to the state capitol. The April rally was one of many held nationwide in what was labeled a National Day of Action to support immigration reform.

In Arizona, at least sixteen immigrant advocacy groups, about sixty evangelical churches, and a weeks-long Spanish and English media campaign had galvanized the demonstrators. Before the march, local community activists from Phoenix and other major cities across the country convened in California, where they formulated strategies to oppose anti-immigrant legislation. Latino youth, including many high school and university students, participated in the event, many of them "DREAMers": undocumented immigrants who had been brought to the United States as small children. Some people criticized the students for missing school; others touted the protests as a great civics lesson. "Many students don't have their papers, but they're good kids with dreams of being somebody," said seventeen-year-old Adrian Mendoza, a student at Metro Tech High School in Phoenix. "They're frustrated with a system that basically says, 'study hard' and then says, 'but you can't get a job because you don't have your papers,' that's why so many of us are protesting" (Meléndez and Hensley 2006).

One of the most notable leaders in the April demonstration was Roberto Reveles, a Latino community activist from Miami, Arizona. A former aide to three members of Congress, in 1972 Roberto Reveles unsuccessfully ran for a seat in the House of Representatives and worked for many years in the energy industry before retiring. "These people are coming across the border for the simple act of providing food and shelter for their families," Reveles said at the time of the march. He mobilized demonstrators through his organization Unidos en Arizona, who, called for a boycott of businesses and was pivotal in generating the attention of more established leaders and lawmakers nationally (González 2006).

Reveles and other organizers felt that it was important for demonstrators to wave American flags, not Mexican flags, and to maintain a pro-American stance, even as they pressed for immigrants' rights. Marchers were also encouraged to wear white t-shirts, to signify solidarity and peace. The marchers needed to be seen as positive, hard-working contributors to the U.S. economy. "We want to demonstrate that we are contributing to this country, and we are helping develop this nation in every aspect," said twenty-four-year-old golf course maintenance worker David Santos, an unauthorized immigrant from Guatemala, who wore an American flag bandana on his head, and another American flag around his shoulders (González et al. 2006).

Latino elected officials and civil rights leaders also marched in the rallies, chanting, "Hoy marchamos, mañana votamos" ("Today we march, tomorrow we vote"). Congressmen Ed Pastor of Phoenix and Raúl Grijalva of Tucson, as well as some prominent state legislators, student leaders from the university, union activists, and church leaders, all spoke at rallies (González et al. 2006).

Demonstrators were urged to channel their energy to create positive change by registering to vote. Former Arizona state senate president Alfredo Gutiérrez ended the rally, declaring, "We shall arm ourselves, and in America, the only weapon that counts is the vote . . . Be prepared to defeat those who humiliate us and defend those who stand with us." Despite the impressive show of people power, efforts to reform the country's immigration policies failed in Congress, although the attempt to make undocumented immigration a felony was thwarted.

Since the 2006 demonstrations, immigrant advocates have been steadily growing the number of registered Latino voters. Community activists worked to capitalize on the newfound energy in the Latino community, while various voter registration drives were carried out throughout Maricopa County, particularly in densely populated Latino districts. Pastors in churches and on Spanish gospel radio urged participation in the mass immigration demonstrations in 2006. One report maintained that in Phoenix Latino evangelical pastors played a major role in recruiting over one hundred thousand demonstrators:

> Some churches sent entire congregations. Others passed out fliers after Sunday services or promoted the rally from behind the pulpit or on Spanish-language Christian radio stations, among them Radio Manantial (91.1 FM) and KASA-AM (1540). There are about 300 evangelical Latino churches in the Valley. About 75 percent of the 15,000 members are unauthorized immigrants, and many have seen family members deported or die crossing the border. (González and Wingett 2006)

Churches have also played an increasingly important role in politically mobilizing Latinos. A growing number of Latinos are no longer just Catholic; protestant and evangelical denominations are making inroads into the Latino immigrant community. These churches provide social support networks for newly arrived immigrants and alternative avenues for political mobilization. Latino evangelicals are a growing constituency in Phoenix, as they are in México and Central and South America (Stoll 1990).

Although often characterized as socially conservative, Latino immigrants are strong advocates of progressive immigration reform policies. Immigrants

Without Borders, a prominent Latino immigrant advocacy group in Arizona, worked with evangelical churches as well as engaged many of the participants in the demonstrations. Indeed, organizers of the demonstrations maintain that Latino evangelical pastors, who are sometimes unauthorized immigrants themselves, played a major role in politically mobilizing the community. In Arizona, Promise Arizona (PAZ), a grassroots community organization aimed at building immigrant and Latino political power, displays the image of the Virgin of Guadalupe for the members of these churches, as well as for the pastors, the immediacy of debates about immigration policy cannot be overstated. For example, José González, pastor of Iglesia Bautista Nuevo Nacimiento, a Latino evangelical church in West Phoenix, said at the time of the demonstration that more than forty evangelical Latino pastors supported the cause: "At first, churches saw this as a political movement, but then we could see our people needed our support. It was a community need. It was beyond politics" (González and Wingett 2006). Magdalena Schwartz, a pastor at Iglesia Palabra de Vida in Mesa, said many evangelical Latino pastors wanted to get involved because not only would the Sensenbrenner Immigration Bill make immigrants criminals, it would also make them very vulnerable to prosecution (2006).

It should be noted that not all evangelicals had taken what might be called a "progressive" position on immigration. Some of the larger, politically influential evangelical organizations remained on the sidelines of the immigration debate during this time, leading to a potential schism between these groups and the Latino evangelical groups. Reverend Samuel Rodríguez, president of the National Latino Christian Leadership Conference, which serves 10,700 Latino evangelical churches with fifteen million members, stated:

> This is the watershed movement—it's the moment where either we really forge relationships with the white evangelical church that will last for decades, or there is a possibility of a definitive schism here . . . there will be church ramifications to this, and there will be political ramifications. . . . So down the road, when the white evangelical community calls us and says, "We want to partner with you on marriage, we want to partner on family issues," my first question will be: "Where were you when 12 million of our brothers and sisters were

about to be deported and 12 million families disenfranchised?" (Cooperman 2006)

Maricopa County and Sheriff Joe

While restrictive anti-immigration policies continued to be enacted at the federal and state levels, the Maricopa County Sheriff's Office (MCSO) had implemented its own immigration policies. From 1993 to 2017, Joe Arpaio, self-proclaimed as "America's Toughest Sheriff," was the head of the MCSO. He was reelected for six four-year terms. During Sheriff Joe Arpaio's final term (2017), there were about 6.5 million people living in Arizona, with Maricopa County being home to about four million of the total population. In this county resides the City of Phoenix, which is now more than 40 percent Latino. Further, the MCSO is the third largest county-wide police department in the nation.

As a sheriff, Joe Arpaio had a long and controversial history, particularly when it came to immigration and the treatment of Latinos. Arpaio is a hero to some Arizonans and a villain to others. After a career in the military and then as a federal narcotics agent, Arpaio wound up in Arizona, where he and his wife ran a travel agency.

Much of the eighty-four-year-old's notoriety stems from his publicity-seeking activities and his tough tactics with inmates. MCSO maintains that Sheriff Joe has been profiled in over 4,500 national and international news outlets. His most noted policies are jailing inmates in outdoor tents in Arizona's blistering heat and making them wear pink underwear and rubber flip-flop sandals, which civil rights advocates say are meant to humiliate prisoners. The MCSO website states that there are between 7,500 to 10,000 inmates in the Arizona jail system at any given time. The MCSO also runs a "chain gang": jail inmates who annually contribute presumably thousands of dollars of free labor, collecting trash on the streets, painting over graffiti, and even burying the indigent in the county cemetery (Arizona State Legislature 2011).

The sheriff had also implemented what he called "get tough" policies on inmates, banning smoking, coffee, movies, pornographic magazines, and unrestricted TV. He claimed that he had instituted the cheapest meals in jails in the United States, by making all meals vegetarian: the average cost of a meal for an inmate in Maricopa jails is between fifteen and forty cents. Inmates are also fed only twice daily, to cut the labor costs of meal delivery. Sheriff Arpaio had even stopped serving salt and pepper to save taxpayers an estimated twenty thousand dollars a year (MCSO 2016). Arpaio had also initiated a mug shot program: each person arrested by the MCSO (at an estimated three hundred persons a day) gets their picture posted on the MCSO website, regardless if the person is later found innocent. The MCSO maintains that the mug shot site is viewed by approximately one million people per day, making it one of the most popular law enforcement sites online (MCSO 2016).

The MCSO has settled millions of dollars in lawsuits, based on multiple allegations of inmate abuse by officers and of poor conditions in the jails, and has been sued over 2,700 times for various reasons, including allegations of cruel treatment to inmates, racial profiling, and illegally carrying out immigration policy. Several families whose loved ones died while in custody have won suits against the MCSO. By the end of 2011, $176 million was being pursued in court over misconduct by the MCSO and another $45 million had already been paid in damages (Biggers 2012). This includes a false-arrest lawsuit settled out of court with the co-founders of the *Phoenix New Times* newspaper. Arpaio had claimed the newspaper, a long-time critic of the sheriff and his policies, violated the law when it published his home address.

Around 2007–8, the MCSO had the most deputies trained through 287(g): approximately 170 in the country. As noted, the 287(g) policy is intended to pursue investigations relating to various criminal offenses, but not immigration enforcement. Under Arpaio, the MCSO implemented highly controversial and contentious programs under the veil of 287(g). Calling the actions "crime suppression sweeps," the MSCO set up "stop-and-detention" checkpoints in predominately Latino communities. Officers would stop Latino residents for minor traffic violations—such as rolling through a stop sign or driving with a broken taillight—and question them regarding their status, and then detain them for an indeterminate amount of time, despite the fact that 287(g)'s provisions stipulate that individuals cannot be targeted for minor offenses. Not surprisingly, there were numerous instances where a parent who was in the country unlawfully went to work and never returned home. There are organizations in Phoenix to call when young children have been separated from their parents because of crime suppression procedures. Needless to say, police officers enforcing immigration policies have destroyed positive relations between police and Latinos. Immigrants will not call the police for help for fear they will be deported.

The MCSO has been under investigation for these practices and has overstepped their boundaries under 287(6) in many other ways. For example, the MCSO arrested a woman because she had an expired license tag. Another woman was holding a garage sale in front of her home when she was arrested for identity theft. The female had shown an expired California driver's license and a Mexican Consular Card. In 2008, MCSO deputies arrested janitors that were working during the night at the City of Mesa library and who had fraudulent documents. When Latino citizens refuse to answer questions regarding their citizenship status, they can be detained for hours. One landscaper was arrested because he could not prove his U.S. citizenship and later released after twelve hours, after proof of his identity was provided.

The activities by the MCSO also impact Latino children. Mary Rose Wilcox, a retired member of the Maricopa County board of supervisors who runs a youth program in Phoenix, says,

> [The program is] for fifth-grade kids who live near the ballpark but would never be able to afford to go to a Diamondbacks baseball game. They all do community-service work, about a thousand of them, and then they get to go to a game. Sheriff's deputies always helped me with the program till two years ago. But I had to ask them to stop. The kids are just too afraid of those brown shirts. That is what their teachers told me. And I hate to say it, but the Sheriff is responsible for all this fear. It's like a big joke to him. He has no idea the harm he's doing to children, families, and communities. (Finnegan 2009)

Most notably, the MCSO has carried out numerous crime sweeps in Guadalupe, a small town in Maricopa County predominately made up of Latinos, both legal and unauthorized, as well as Yaqui and other Native Americans. Since Guadalupe does not have its own police agency, the town has a contract with the MCSO. In this community, the MCSO has stopped and asked for the identification of citizens and anyone that looked "foreign" for identification. If the individual failed to provide documentation, they were arrested. The MCSO maintained that it was asked by the town leaders to perform crime suppression sweeps. However, at no time could proof of such requests be provided by MCSO.

In 2009, a report to Homeland Security, produced by the Government Accountability Office (GAO), regarding the national impact of 287(g) found that some police departments across the country were focused on minor violations rather than on serious offenses when implementing the law (Aizenman 2009). Further, in a study by the Goldwater Institute, a research center in Phoenix, scholars found that MCSO policies of immigration enforcement have been highly ineffective and deter officers from pursuing more important law enforcement activities. The MCSO would arrest only low-level operatives, such as drivers and drop-house guards. More important, the report noted that 287(g) had diverted substantial resources and time away from other law enforcement activities: the sweeps had involved a substantial number of deputies that were not trained to implement the policy and the response time to 911 calls had increased (Bolick 2008).

Not all police agencies in Arizona chose to use 287(g) money. These agencies wanted to maintain a good relationship with the Latino community; they did not want Latinos that were in the country unlawfully to be afraid to call for assistance. One assistant chief of police from the Tucson region even felt that his agency was punished by the state legislature for not taking 287(g) federal money, because there is a real pressure to get extra funding.

In 2007, Arizona governor Janet Napolitano signed House Bill 2779, an Arizona employers sanctions law that took effect in January 2008. Essentially the law requires employers to verify that their employees are in the country legally. If an employer knowingly hires an unauthorized worker, they are subject to a ten-day suspension of their business license; a second offense can result in its permanent revocation. Verification of a worker's status is made via the Employment Eligibility Verification System (EEV), commonly known as E-Verify. If an employee is in the country illegally or their status cannot be verified, the employer receives a "Notice of Suspect Documents." Employers are then considered informed and must terminate employment as well as not rehire the employee in the future. Employers can also choose not to use the E-Verify system. In 2011, the Supreme Court upheld Arizona's Employer Sanctions law because it targets businesses, maintaining that the state is not passing an immigration law or trying to control immigration.

Russell Pearce

While anti-immigration fervor had continued to grow in Arizona, another key political actor took the stage. The ascent of state senator Russell Pearce to power in Arizona in 2006 paralleled a growing nationwide backlash against progressive policies such as affirmative action, bilingual education, and a woman's right to choose. Pearce opposed those policies as well, but his obsession and path to power was his opposition to immigration, particularly the immigration of Mexican immigrants.

In Pearce's view, Mexican and other Latin American immigrants were fundamentally incapable of becoming full-fledged, law-abiding Americans. His mantra—"What part of illegal don't you understand?"—was intended as more than a simple condemnation of immigrants who had violated federal civil statutes by entering the United States undocumented: it was a nativist call to arms. Underlying the statement was always the implication that immigrants, by coming to the United States without documentation, no matter what their motivation, were a threat to the American way of life—namely, the ultraconservative American way of life, as defined by Pearce and his fellow nativists.

As a demagogue, Pearce was Arizona's Joseph McCarthy, except that the threat to what he described as "the America I know" was not communism, but immigration and the "brown hoards." Pearce came to the elected office in Arizona at precisely the right place at the right time to pursue his anti-immigrant agenda. Of significance is that Pearce was a passionate political ally of Maricopa County Sheriff Joe Arpaio; he once served as Arpaio's chief deputy.

Russell Pearce began his career as a MCSO deputy, a position he held for twenty-three years, working under the supervision of Sheriff Joe Arpaio. In 1995, he became the director of the Arizona Motor Vehicle Department. As director, he implemented a program that required an individual to provide a social security number when applying for an Arizona driver's license, which means that a person could not get a driver's license if they were in the country unlawfully.

In 2000, Pearce was elected to the Arizona House of Representatives. The city of Mesa, the second-largest city in Arizona, was in his district. The City of Mesa has a significant Mormon population, and Pearce is himself a Mormon. In 2004, Pearce was a vocal supporter of proposition 200, the policy that discourages unauthorized immigrants to vote or use welfare, even though they were not permitted to do so. In 2006, Pearce was elected to the state senate. During his political career, he has publicly made many anti-immigrant comments. He generated national notoriety for stating on NPR that Arizona needed to bring back another Operation Wetback Program, the massive deportation program from the 1950s. In 2008, Pearce introduced legislation that would ban education programs that did not support American values. He also proposed legislation that would deny birthright citizenship to children whose parents are unauthorized immigrants, maintaining that Mexican immigrants come to the United States to have babies that he referred to as "anchor babies." As Pearce rose to power to become state senate president, some suggested he was more powerful than the sitting governor, Jan Brewer. Evidence abounded, as far as Pearce was concerned, that the "brown hoards" he had read about in the Book of Mormon were taking over. Between 1990 and 2010, the number of Latinos in Arizona had nearly tripled, though this was mostly due to population growth among native-born Latinos and not immigration (Pew Research Center Hispanic Trends 2020). Latinos, who made up 18.8 percent of the population in 1990, made up 30 percent in 2010 (US Census Bureau 1990). Further, the foreign-born community of Arizona only consisted of approximately 13 percent of the total population, while the native-born made up 16 percent (Pew Research Center Hispanic Trends 2012a, 2012b). As Pearce and Arpaio gained power, a movement in California to ban bilingual education and affirmative action, primarily as a backlash to rapid Latino population growth there, had spread to Arizona. Couple this with the implementation of a U.S. Border Patrol plan that clamped down on border crossings by undocumented immigrants in Southern California and Texas—which effectively funneled immigrants into a smuggling corridor that led through Phoenix—and Pearce had all the ammunition he needed to claim that Arizona (and, by extension, America) was being "invaded."

It was irrelevant to Pearce that the vast majority of immigrants coming across the border were escaping abject poverty in their homelands to better their lives in a nation with a thriving economy and in desperate need of immigrant labor. His argument against immigration had virtually nothing to do with economics, though he routinely echoed the hollow claim that immigrants were taking jobs from American workers. Almost exclusively, when Pearce talked about immigrants who crossed the Mexican border, he made it a point to describe them as law-breaking, disease-ridden, and depraved.

Among Pearce's common refrains were his false assertions of an epidemic rate of tuberculosis among undocumented immigrants and that thousands of child molesters were part of the immigrant wave. In one particularly illustrative example, he falsely claimed that the greatest number of murderers in federal prison were Mexican immigrants. Confronted by journalists, Pearce attributed the claim to a press release by U.S. congressman Steven King. Congressman King's claim—which he had inaccurately extrapolated from a government report about the number of immigrants being housed in federal prison—was ultimately discredited.

Pearce's rise to power not only paralleled immigration trends nationwide and the growing conservatism of Arizona voters, much of it linked to an influx of Californians and Midwesterners, it also arrived in the wake of the 9/11 attacks. Even though none of the terrorists who attacked the United States that day were from México or Latin America nor had they crossed the U.S.-México border, Pearce and other conservative politicians spoke often of the purported terrorist threat posed by America's "porous" southwest border.

Also important is that Pearce's election as state senate president also coincided with the Great Recession. Arizona's economy was one of the most impacted in the nation, in large part because of the state's dependence on the housing-construction industry, which was widely known to hire undocumented workers. Concurrently, growing anti-immigrant sentiment in the state and the ascent of Pearce and his allies all combined to make life miserable not only for undocumented immigrants, but many documented immigrants and even U.S.-born Latinos, some of whom were victimized by the racial profiling practices of the MCSO.

In 2009, prominent Latino leaders convened to discuss the ever-increasing attacks on immigrants in Arizona. "It's more subtle than it used to be," said Daniel Ortega, a leading civil rights attorney and community activist in Phoenix who made national headlines when he stated, "We find ourselves, as

Latinos, whether documented or not, in a social situation in which our civil rights are not being respected." He maintained that public officials, like Maricopa County sheriff Joe Arpaio and state senator Russell Pearce, are using the political system in ways that ultimately, even if less overtly, discriminate against Latinos, in a manipulation of public policy that has stoked public discontent with immigrants. By spreading misinformation, Ortega asserts, Pearce and his allies have perpetuated a culture of fear among Latinos and fueled a growing hostility toward Latino immigrants and Latinos in general.

Enter Senate Bill 1070

In 2010, senator Russell Pearce and state representative John Kavanagh cosponsored Senate Bill 1070. Representative John Kavanagh had maintained on numerous occasions that unauthorized immigrants were committing a significant number of dangerous crimes in the state, such as kidnapping, and that they drained public services. Pearce and Kavanagh's intent with SB 1070 was to curb immigration through intimidation tactics.

Involved in the backing of SB 1070 was the Federation for American Immigration Reform (FAIR), the organization that helped to fund Proposition 187 in California in 1994 and Proposition 200 in 2004 in Arizona. The Southern Poverty Law Center says the following regarding FAIR:

> The Federation for American Immigration Reform (FAIR) is a group with one mission: to severely limit immigration into the United States. Although FAIR maintains a veneer of legitimacy that has allowed its principals to testify in Congress and lobby the federal government, this veneer hides much ugliness. FAIR leaders have ties to white supremacist groups and eugenicists and have made many racist statements. Its advertisements have been rejected because of racist content. FAIR's founder, John Tanton, has expressed his wish that America remain a majority-white population: a goal to be achieved, presumably, by limiting the number of nonwhites who enter the country. One of the group's main goals is upending the Immigration and Nationality Act of 1965, which ended a decades-long, racist quota system that limited immigration mostly to northern Europeans. FAIR President Dan Stein has called the Act a "mistake." (2016)

Arizona gained national attention with the adoption of SB 1070, which contained numerous anti-immigration and race-based provisions (Bebout 2016). This legislation will be discussed in more detail later in this book, but the following summarizes the most controversial provisions contained in the law. First, it not only made it a violation of state law to be in the United States without legal status; it also extended the authority of local law enforcement "to stop and verify the immigration status of anyone they suspected of being undocumented" (Ciment and Radzilowski 2014) and to conduct a warrantless arrest. Further, police were *required*, during normal investigations, to inquire about immigration status and to ask for citizenship paperwork if they had any doubt that a person was in the U.S. illegally (2014). In other words, it was mandatory for officers to make an attempt to determine the immigration status of a person stopped, detained, or arrested for reasonable suspicion of their legal status.

In addition, SB 1070 made it a separate state offense, with criminal penalties, to violate the federal immigration law regarding registration and the carrying of registration documents, making it a state crime for someone to not carry their alien-registration papers. It was also a violation of the law for unauthorized immigrants to solicit, apply for, or perform work. An undocumented person could not proposition for work in any public place, such as through gesture or a nod. What's more, anyone who attempted to hire or pick up day laborers would be considered to be impeding the normal flow of traffic and subject to jail time. If day laborers did enter the car, SB 1070 mandated the impoundment of any vehicle to transport, move, conceal, harbor, or shield an unauthorized immigrant (Alto Arizona! n.d.).

Law enforcement—whether they agreed with the provisions or not—were required to enforce the federal immigration laws to the fullest extent of the law. If they failed to do so, or if a person perceived that law enforcement officials failed to do so, SB 1070 created a private right of action for the individual to sue the city, town, or county for neglecting federal immigration laws (Alto Arizona! n.d.). This created an atmosphere of "someone is always watching" and was used to ensure that the anti-immigration measures were being executed. Finally, the legislation strengthened the state's employer sanctions laws, giving prosecutors more latitude in investigations. The policy was amended and then went to the Senate, where the revised bill passed by seventeen (Republicans) to eleven (Democrats). Only one Republican chose not to vote for the bill. Ten Democrats opposed the bill while two chose not to vote.

When governor Janet Napolitano left Arizona to be the head of the newly established Department of Homeland Security in 2008, Jan Brewer was the state secretary at the time and second in line to the governor. In 2010, when she ran for reelection, her popularity was low. All was not necessarily right in conservative GOP circles. Brewer and Pearce were often at odds. While Brewer rarely appeared in public with Pearce, she quickly adopted his rhetoric on immigration, once going so far as to erroneously claiming that "a majority" of undocumented immigrants were drug mules. Brewer and Pearce also supported voter-approved state legislation that prohibited all undocumented immigrants from receiving in-state tuition and agreed on requiring that the state's voters show photo identification when casting a ballot.

When Governor Brewer signed SB 1070, polling showed that her support for the bill and her anti-immigrant rhetoric boosted her popularity with many Arizonans. Surveys found that around 70 percent of non-Latino Arizona voters supported policies like SB 1070 (Camarota 2010). However, when registered Latino voters in Arizona were asked if they supported the law, a whopping 86 percent opposed it.

Governor Brewer maintained that immigration was out of control in Arizona. She claimed that, because of escalating violence and drug smuggling in México, Arizona law enforcement agents had found numerous beheaded bodies in the desert. When challenged by reporters for proof, she later recanted her comments, maintaining she misspoke. On other occasions, Governor Brewer claimed that the majority of undocumented immigrants entering Arizona were under the control of organized drug cartels and delivering drugs to the United States (Jacobson 2010). These comments may have helped get her reelected, but it hurt the state's reputation. Businesses chose not to come to Arizona because the rhetoric of public officials made the state look unsafe.

Not everyone was on board with the punitive stance toward immigrants. For instance, when SB 1070 was under consideration, some police officers in Arizona did not want to carry it out because it would ruin relationships in the Latino community. Numerous interviews with border patrol representatives, police officers, and policy makers revealed the belief that many of the policies linked to the immigration crackdown—which they considered poorly written, largely symbolic, and practically impossible to implement—were part of an anti-immigrant agenda created to appease conservative constituents.

SB 1070 was immediately challenged by a broad coalition of groups, including the American Civil Liberties Union, Mexican American Legal Defense and Educational Fund, National Immigration Law Center, National Association for the Advancement of Colored People, ACLU of Arizona, National Day Laborer Organizing Network, and the Asian Pacific American Legal Center. The lawsuits charged that the Arizona law interferes with federal authority over immigration, violates the supremacy clause of the U.S. Constitution, invites racial profiling, and infringes on the free speech of immigrants in Arizona. Several prominent law enforcement groups, including the Arizona Association of Chiefs of Police, opposed the law because it diverts limited resources from law enforcement's responsibility and destroys police-citizen relationships that are integral when policing diverse communities. The U.S. Department of Justice also brought suit, stating that the state law violated federal law.

On July 28, 2010, Judge Susan Bolton ruled for a temporary injunction on four of the law's provisions: officers do not have to make a reasonable attempt to determine the immigration status of a person stopped, detained or arrested if there is a reasonable suspicion that they are in the country illegally; it will not be a crime if you are not carrying an alien-registration papers; officers cannot make warrantless arrests of persons; and it is not a crime for illegal immigrants to solicit, apply for, or perform work. What has gone into effect and is not temporarily stopped: it is a crime to pick up a day laborer in a roadway if stopping impedes traffic; law enforcement still must enforce federal immigration laws to the fullest extent of the law; and individuals will still be able to sue an agency if it is perceived that it is not enforcing the law.

Governor Brewer remarked that the judge's ruling "was a little bump in the road," and Sheriff Arpaio said that he was not surprised by Bolton's ruling, while maintaining that it would have little impact on his planned crime-suppression operations. The Ninth Circuit Court upheld the injunction in April 2011. Arizona later appealed the decision to the U.S. Supreme Court, which heard arguments by the state and the Justice Department on

April 25, 2012. In June 2012, the U.S. Supreme Court overturned most parts of the bill, except for the provision that requires police officers to make a reasonable attempt when determining the immigration status of a person stopped, detained, or arrested. The Court also maintained that there must be reasonable suspicion that the person is in the country illegally. Most important, the Court stated that it would reconsider its decision if civil rights violations took place.

On September 2012, the American Civil Liberties Union, the National Immigration Law Center, and the Mexican American Legal Defense and Educational Fund requested that a new injunction be placed on the law after the Supreme Court's ruling. The plaintiffs maintained that the law encourages the lengthy detention of people with a Latino phenotype and that the law violated the Equal Protection Clause of the Fourteenth Amendment. Judge Susan Bolton declined to issue a new injunction.

In *League of United Latin American Citizens (LULAC) v. State of Arizona*, LULAC joined with a few residents of Arizona to point out portions of the law that should be deemed unconstitutional. Joining LULAC in the suit were Anna Ochoa O'Leary and Cordelia Chávez Candelaria Beveridge, both American citizens; Magdalena Schwartz (citizen of Chile); José David Sandoval (citizen of El Salvador); and three Mexican nationals. All plaintiffs external to LULAC were residents of Arizona and had individual complaints with SB 1070, ranging from state expenditures on the law to inability to legally gain asylum. The plaintiffs claimed that the law violated the Supremacy, Interstate Commerce, and Due Process clauses of the U.S. Constitution.

Filed in April 2010 by two nonprofit organizations affiliated with over thirty thousand churches, three hundred Arizona pastors, and other citizens, *National Coalition of Latino Clergy and Christian Leaders v. State of Arizona* extended the suit to "all persons who currently reside in Arizona and are negatively affected by the proposed unconstitutional law." This lawsuit looked again to Due Process and the Supremacy Clause, but also the First Amendment. Many other lawsuits were filed against the State of Arizona and against Governor Brewer herself. Most of these challenged the constitutionality of SB 1070 or voiced legal issues that resulted from the law's passage.

SB 1070 marked the pinnacle of Pearce's power and the beginning of his political downfall. Anti-immigration groups nationwide were emboldened by the passing of the legislation, and hundreds of anti-immigration bills inspired by 1070 were proposed in state legislatures nationwide in the ensuing months and years. While these failed, nationally, the anti-immigration sentiment had shifted away from federal efforts to reform U.S. immigration policy and to state-based legislation. By the time SB 1070 was signed into law by Governor Brewer in 2010, Pearce (along with Sheriff Arpaio) had become a darling of right-wing conservative news media outlets, such as the twenty-four-hour Fox News.

CHAPTER 3

Political Backlash

When Arizona governor Jan Brewer signed SB 1070 in Phoenix, hundreds of demonstrations took place locally, nationally, and internationally, most of them a week before and after the passage of the bill. Some of the prominent players in Arizona that toiled in 2006 to oppose anti-immigrant legislation were back in the spotlight again, and several organizations—both formal and informal—were created to oppose anti-immigration. Economic boycotts also ensued.

There were several marches in Maricopa County— most notably, a five-mile walk to downtown Phoenix, where the state capitol and the Maricopa County Sheriff's Office (MCSO) are located. Estimates of attendance for these various marches ranged from thirty thousand to one hundred thousand. Some witnesses noted that many students walked out of class from schools across the State of Arizona in order to participate. Isabel García, an immigrant activist from the Coalición de Derechos Humanos, said, "The youth are fearless, the youth have a political analysis that few adults have. We urge churches, unions and mainstream organizations to pay attention" (Hing 2010). One student named Luis maintained that "it's possible that he and other students could be suspended for ditching school to take part in the protest, but it's a risk they're willing to take" (2010).

At one of the rallies, the MCSO arrested over fifty demonstrators, some of them prominent leaders and immigrant activists, including Alfredo Gutiérrez and Salvador Reza, as well as a photographer for the *Arizona Republic*, the largest newspaper in the state. Sheriff Joe Arpaio was quoted as saying, "My deputies will arrest them and put them in pink underwear" (King 2010).

Elected Officials

Prominent elected leaders convened at several rallies at the state capitol. Congressman Raúl Grijalva (D-AZ) who since 2003 has represented Arizona's Third Congressional District, an area near Tucson, is a staunch advocate for the environment as well as for immigration reform. According to Daniel Levine of news website Heavy.com, after Governor Brewer signed SB 1070 into law she said, "Being a first-generation American, having had to deal with the consequences of being an immigrant family to all of a sudden have a law that separates me from the whole, I found very offensive and demeaning . . . it is personal" (2017). Representative Grijalva was the first to call for boycotting the state, releasing a statement asking organizations to hold off on scheduling any conventions in Arizona, since conventions are a large source of tourism and revenue. The boycotts lasted sixteen months and were estimated to have cost Arizona millions in lost revenues.

Some leaders debated if boycotts were wise, given that they hurt immigrant workers. CPLC did not support the boycotts for this reason. The Arizona Chamber of Commerce did not support SB 1070 either, but it also did not support the boycotts. Congressman Ed Pastor, also a fellow Democrat, called for the law to be repealed, but did not support the boycotts. Representative Gabby Giffords (D-AZ) did not support SB 1070, but she did not overtly oppose it, maintaining that her constituents needed something to be done about immigration.

The call for boycotts had a negative effect on Grijalva's reelection. In 2010, after Grijalva backed the boycotts, the congressman faced his closest election ever, due to declining support. Although he had always received around 60 percent of the vote, he was only one or two points ahead of his opponent in the 2010 campaign. Voters reacted mostly to the boycott and not necessarily positively to Republican front-runner Ruth McClung. Ultimately, Grijalva was able to secure reelection, but only by a small margin (Riccardi 2010).

Pastor maintained that "Arizona is better than this," and "it's embarrassing to continue to see [Arizona's] state legislature churn out these hate-filled measures that offer no real solutions and violate our civil rights." Pastor spoke at a protest—one of the largest—in front of the Arizona state capitol in May 2010, organized by the National Day Laborer Organizing Network and that included a five-mile march through Phoenix by tens of thousands of participants. Pastor and Grijalva were the only two Arizona congressmen to even speak out against SB 1070. There was a remarkable lack of vocal opposition to SB 1070 from many of Arizona's elected officials.

Interestingly, a congressman from Illinois, Luis Gutiérrez (D-IL), brought a greater national presence to Arizona by expressing his opposition to SB 1070. Gutiérrez, who is of Puerto Rican decent and one of the first Latino congress members to be elected in the Midwest, made SB 1070 and immigration a national issue for Latinos. An advocate for defending immigrants' rights as well as a path to citizenship for unauthorized immigrants, Gutiérrez has been elected to Congress eleven times, first in 1992. Interestingly, though his family is from Puerto Rico, and he never personally dealt with issues of immigration due to the fact that Puerto Ricans are U.S. citizens, regardless of their being born in Puerto Rico or on the mainland, he became engaged with the agenda due to the problems that his friends and colleagues confronted (Ciment and Radzilowski 2014).

In 1993, Gutiérrez established workshops to help Latinos gain citizenship in his home district of Chicago. According to his official website, "As of 2014, more than 55,000 constituents had received assistance to make the transition from legal permanent resident to citizen of the United States." Gutiérrez also introduced legislation that would later become the DREAM Act. His proposed bill, the Immigrant Children's Educational Advantage and Dropout Prevention Act (HR 1582), would grant legal status to all minors who have lived in the United States for at least five years and who are currently a student (Gutiérrez 2016).

Although the House failed to vote on much of his legislation, the congressman continues to be the most vocal advocate for immigration. Gutiérrez also pushed for legislation that would prevent the separation of families after President Obama announced the Deferred Action for Childhood Arrivals (DACA). In "Pick Out the Immigrant," a famous speech made to the House on June 27, 2012, he compared well-known figures like Justin Bieber, Selena Gómez, Jeremy Lin, and Tony Parker as well as Supreme Court Justices Antonin Scalia and Sonia Sotomayor to one another, noting that they were most likely immigrants or children of immigrants. He noted that, "maybe with practice, we can become like Arizona politicians and police officers who are able to telepathically determine who to accuse of not belonging in America" (Gutiérrez 2016).

Finally, Gutiérrez has been outspoken about Republicans' stagnancy on immigration reform and at times even about President Obama's silence on the matter. In his autobiography, *Still Dreaming: My Journey from the Barrio to Capitol Hill*, Gutiérrez criticizes the president for not fulfilling his campaign promises of reforming immigration. He wrote that Obama "hadn't lifted a finger" toward reform six months into his first term (2016). In 2010, he and other Latino lawmakers considered blocking Obamacare to coerce the president into backing immigration reform.

In October 2013, frustrated over the lack of progress on immigration reform, Gutiérrez and seven other members of Congress participated in the Camino Americano March for Immigration Reform. Led by the National Hispanic Foundation for the Arts, CASA de Maryland, and other organizations, the protest brought thousands of participants to Capitol Hill on October 8, 2013. There, Gutiérrez stated "Our communities and our families do not have the luxury to rest or relax. 1,100 people will be deported today, 1,100 people will be deported tomorrow, and the next day" (Hickson 2013). Representatives John Lewis (D-GA), Charlie Rangel (D-NY), Raúl Grijalva (D-AZ), Joe Crowley (D-NY), Jan Schakowsky (D-IL), Keith Ellison (D-MN), and Al Green (D-TX), and Gutiérrez were all arrested.

Economic Boycotts

After SB 1070, several cities boycotted the law. According to L.A. councilwoman Janice Hahn, "When people are asked to show their papers, it brings back memories of Nazi Germany" (Gorman 2010). In San Francisco, mayor Gavin Newsom suspended city-related travel to Arizona. Darrell Steinberg (D-Sacramento), leader of the California Senate, also came out against SB 1070, asking then-governor Arnold Schwarzenegger for a list of all Arizona businesses and government agencies and proposed an economic boycott. In a letter to Governor Schwarzenegger he stated, "The state of California should not be using taxpayer dollars to support such a policy" (McGreevy 2010).

Congressman José Serrano of New York, who is also Puerto Rican, asked if the 2011 Major League Baseball (MLB) All-Star Game that was to be held in Phoenix could be moved to another state. He maintained that many of the baseball fans and players are of Latin American descent, and that it was disrespectful to hold the event in a state that supported anti-Latino legislation. Also, the World Boxing Council no longer allowed professional boxers to compete in Arizona (MPI 2010). In late April 2010, the executive director of the MLB's player union, Michael Weiner, stated that the law "could have a negative impact on hundreds of major league players" and supported that it be "repealed or modified promptly" (Gorman and Ricardi 2010). According to Weiner, players on the Arizona Diamondbacks and on any team playing in Phoenix run the risk of being adversely affected. The Angels' pitcher Joe Saunders stated to the players' union, on behalf of his team (which he represents for the union), "We're behind you guys 100%." Then L.A. Angels' right fielder Bobby Abreu, who was born in Venezuela, stated, "You're not going to be on the street every time with your passport because you're afraid you might lose it" (Gorman and Riccardi 2010).

MLB players, including Padres first baseman Adrián González and San Diego catcher Yorvit Torrealba, voiced to news reporters their opposition to the law. Additionally, White Sox manager Ozzie Guillen stated that he would boycott the 2011 All Star game, "as a Latin American" (Biggers 2012). Ultimately, in July 2011, none of the players or officials boycotted the game. Many of the Latino baseball players were, again, from other countries than México. And, again, they maintained that they felt a connection to the immigrants who were being targeted.

In opposition to SB 1070, the National Basketball Association's (NBA) Phoenix Suns wore their "Los Suns" jerseys, typically used for the league's "Noche Latina" program on Cinco de Mayo 2010. Suns owner Robert Sarver announced, "Our players and organization felt that wearing our 'Los Suns' jerseys on Cinco de Mayo was a way for our team and our organization to honor our Latino community and the diversity of our league, the State of Arizona, and our nation" (Adande 2010). The team was criticized for taking a public stance on SB 1070.

Various artists publicly opposed the law. Internationally recognized singer Shakira, who is Colombian, came to Arizona and asked to meet with Governor Brewer. The governor declined. Shakira visited Phoenix mayor Phil Gordon and expressed concern over the law, and she later reported that the mayor and chief of police were worried about SB 1070's potential impact on Latino families in Arizona. After speaking with some victims of domestic violence, she reported to CNN that "they're going to live in fear to call the police or to report a crime that has been inflicted to them. They're trying to protect their kids and their own families from abusers and now they're going to have to protect themselves from the government" (CNN 2010). Shakira also stated that if she were stopped by law enforcement in Arizona at the time, she could have been arrested for lack of any documentation.

In what was known as the "Sound Strike," musicians across the country refused to perform in Arizona after SB 1070's passage, including Kanye West, Zach de la Rocha, Pitbull, and the Mexican group Los Tigres del Norte, among hundreds of others. The movement began with an announcement from Rage Against the Machine's lead singer, Zack de la Rocha: "Fans of our music, our stories, our films and our words can be pulled over and harassed every day because they are brown or black, or for the way they speak, or for the music they listen to" (2010). The boycott rapidly gained popularity, joined by Sonic Youth, Tenacious D, Nine Inch Nails, Maroon 5, and My Chemical Romance, to name but a few artists. In México City, 85,000 people attended a concert played by the bands Molotov, Jaguares, and Vecindad in protest of SB 1070 and in support of Latino Arizonans.

When Judge Susan Bolton issued a preliminary injunction against some of the major provisions of SB 1070, the Sound Strike issued a press release, stating that, "until a final decision or until Arizona repeals the law, the artists of Sound Strike stand in firm opposition to the discriminatory and punitive measures of SB 1070" (de la Rocha 2010). Later, the Sound Strike collaborated with the Puente Human Rights Movement (Puente), Alto Arizona, and other organizations to distribute food and toys to families affected by deportation. The group also raised $400,000 for immigration groups in Arizona. Sound Strike organizer Javier González had commented in 2011 that major legislation and/or organizational changes would need to take place before the boycott would be discontinued. Performers gradually returned to Arizona.

The Recall of Russell Pearce

The rise of Russell Pearce and the passage of SB 1070 inspired a powerful reaction from political progressives, civil rights and human rights groups, and immigrant activists both nationally and internationally. In Arizona, grassroots organizations such as Promise Arizona (PAZ) and Mi Familia Vota began organizing against Senator Pearce and Sheriff Arpaio, among others who supported their immigration agenda.

National civil rights groups and civic engagement groups boosted funding for local grassroots organizations. Media outlets from across the nation and around the world described the legislation as the toughest of its kind in the country. Frightfully aware of the economic damage being done to the state as a result of its new unwanted status as the "new Alabama," Arizona business groups, including all of the major chambers of commerce, began to quietly distance themselves from Russell Pearce and Jan Brewer, even as they began backing candidates against anti-immigrant candidates like Pearce.

A handful of business leaders began speaking out against the legislation by arguing that it was "bad for business." The Arizona Hispanic Chamber of Commerce joined a lawsuit filed by the Mexican American Legal Defense and Educational Fund and the American Civil Liberties Union of Arizona. Few individual business leaders, however, dared openly criticize Governor Brewer, fearing that it might negatively impact her generally pro-business stance. One Brewer ally, former attorney general Grant Woods, a Republican, was a vocal critic of the bill, but he also served as Brewer's campaign cochair.

In short order, however, Pearce would find himself on the defensive and struggling to stay in power. Liberal grassroots groups, angered by what they perceived as an all-out assault on immigrants and their families, began to step up mobilization efforts against him. For his part, Pearce would become the first sitting state senate president recalled from office.

Citizens for a Better Arizona (CBA), founded and led by one-time U.S. Senate candidate Randy Parraz, organized the recall campaign and helped inspire tens of thousands of voters, including many Latinos, to mobilize and vote against Pearce. Pearce also met stiff resistance from Arizona's influential Mormon community. While Pearce had claimed publicly that the church supported his stance on immigration, Mormon leaders grumbled in private—since the church is notoriously low-key in its partisan political activities in Arizona—that Pearce had fast become an embarrassment to the church. Church leaders vehemently disputed his claim, even going so far as to recruit Arizona attorney Daryl Williams to publicly discredit Pearce's anti-immigrant rhetoric. Williams visited with local community and church leaders, including many in Pearce's legislative district, to challenge Pearce's ideology. While Williams compared SB 1070 to "bad laws" such as the Alabama laws that prohibited Rosa Parks from sitting with whites on a city bus, the Mormon church also had its own long-term interest in mind by standing against harsh immigration laws: a majority of Mormons around the world speak Spanish as their primary language.

Republican strategist Nathan Sproul stated, "Russell Pearce was making [the Mormon church's] missionary efforts in Central and South America more difficult" (Weiner 2011). Pearce's anti-immigration rhetoric was also making it difficult for the Mormon church to send missions abroad and to reach Hispanic Mormons. Opposing Pearce's stand on immigration, in 2010 the Mormon church signed the Utah Compact, which announced immigration reform beyond solely enforcement:

THE UTAH COMPACT:

A declaration of five principles to guide Utah's immigration discussion

FEDERAL SOLUTIONS Immigration is a federal policy issue between the U.S. government and other countries—not Utah and other countries. We urge Utah's congressional delegation, and others, to lead efforts to strengthen federal laws and protect our national borders. We urge state leaders to adopt reasonable policies addressing immigrants in Utah.

LAW ENFORCEMENT We respect the rule of law and support law enforcement's professional judgment and discretion. Local law enforcement resources should focus on criminal activities, not civil violations of federal code.

FAMILIES Strong families are the foundation of successful communities. We oppose policies that unnecessarily separate families. We champion policies that support families and improve the health, education and well-being of all Utah children.

ECONOMY Utah is best served by a free-market philosophy that maximizes individual freedom and opportunity. We acknowledge the economic role immigrants play as workers and taxpayers. Utah's immigration policies must reaffirm our global reputation as a welcoming and business-friendly state.

A FREE SOCIETY Immigrants are integrated into communities across Utah. We must adopt a humane approach to this reality, reflecting our unique culture, history and spirit of inclusion. The way we treat immigrants will say more about us as a free society and less about our immigrant neighbors. Utah should always be a place that welcomes people of goodwill. ("Utah Compact" 2019)

A frequent guest on conservative twenty-four-hour cable network Fox News, Pearce had become a household name among Tea Party anti-immigrant activists nationwide. However, he had overestimated his degree of support in Arizona, including his own district, for his anti-immigrant agenda. While statewide and national polls had shown widespread support for SB 1070, voters were generally uninformed about many of the particulars of the law.

Pearce's close and often public ties to white supremacist organizations and neo-Nazi supporters had drawn headlines as well. The Fox News affiliate in Phoenix reported on his links to neo-Nazi hate groups. J. T. Ready, an avowed white supremacist and friend of Pearce, had committed a multiple murder before taking his own life, and Pearce once forwarded an email from a virulent anti-Semitic group called the National Alliance, though Pearce claimed he did not read the email before forwarding it.

Citizens for a Better Arizona circulated petitions to have Pearce recalled and by May 2011 had collected over 18,000 signatures in support of the recall. Although a percentage of them had to be considered invalid, only 7,756 were necessary to force a recall election. After the secretary of state's office confirmed the submission of sufficient signatures, Governor Brewer officially called for a recall election on July 12, 2011. As per state law, the election was to be held November 8, 2011. Businessman Jerry Lewis, also a Mormon and a former accountant and charter school administrator, challenged Pearce in the recall election. A moderate Republican, Lewis had publicly and passionately declared his opposition to SB 1070 and the state's growing anti-immigrant mood.

Although the opposition to Pearce centered on his anti-immigrant agenda, there were other issues. First, he was accused of accepting nearly $40,000 worth of tickets and trips from the Fiesta Bowl. Accepting the tickets and trips was considered unlawful, although no legal action was taken.

Incredibly, during Pearce's recall election, a sham candidate was intentionally placed on the ballot, to reduce the number of votes that would go to Russell Pearce's opponent, Jerry Lewis. Olivia Cortes (note the intentional Spanish surname) was a naturalized immigrant from México who entered the recall election as another Republican on the ballot. After announcing her candidacy, however, she made no attempts to campaign and held no fundraisers. She also never participated in the local GOP groups. In the end, it turned out that Cortes's involvement in the election was indeed solely an effort to try and take away votes—especially Latino votes—from Lewis. Randy Parraz, a member of the Citizens for a Better Arizona group and one of the main organizers of the petition for the recall, said at a press conference that Olivia Cortes was a supporter of Russell Pearce. The candidate dropped out of the race.

It was later found out that Russell Pearce's brother, justice of the peace Lester Pearce, had carried signs in support of his brother in an attempt to sway voters. Justice Pearce's daughter, Megan Sirrine, obtained signatures for Olivia Cortes. Another of Russell Pearce's nieces, Shilo Sessions, was reported to have circulated petitions for Cortes, despite having signs supporting Russell Pearce on her lawn. Cortes, under oath, denied having any idea who circulated petitions for her, who paid for her campaign signs, or who designed and managed her campaign website. She maintained that the reason she remained mostly hidden from the public eye was that she was simply a private person.

Jerry Lewis defeated Russell Pearce in the state's first recall election with 53.4 percent of the vote versus Pearce's 45.4 percent. Pearce was forced to concede the race. His campaign manager stated that this race had "set a dangerous precedent," because the recall campaign took a look at the numbers and decided to "find a white, Mormon, male Republican candidate to run against Russell to split that vote." Jerry Lewis said,

> The biggest hurdle for Arizona to get over was just what happened. Mr. Pearce was the man. He was SB 1070. He was the president of the Senate, the architect of that bill and that was his claim to fame. That message was defeated tonight. I don't think there is anything. . . . Arizona could've done more significant than this. This is a huge shift, maintained Parraz shortly after the 2011 election. This election shows that such extremist behavior will not be rewarded and will be held accountable. (Montero 2011)

Grassroots Activism

Much of the success of the campaign against Pearce was due in significant ways to the participation of young DREAMers: young undocumented immigrants who had been brought to the United States as children and who were part of groups such as Team Awesome and Promise Arizona (PAZ), armed with computer-generated lists of targeted registered voters as part of a door-to-door campaign to recall Pearce. These immigrant activists also helped elect Phoenix mayor Greg Stanton and Latino Phoenix council members Daniel Valenzuela and Michael Nowakowski. With the election of Valenzuela, the Phoenix City Council had for the first time two Latino council members. In Valenzuela's district alone, partly due to the efforts of Team Awesome, Latino voter turnout grew nearly five-fold.

Team Awesome consisted of a group of dozens of community volunteers, mainly students from the west side of Phoenix. These individuals were committed to promoting civic engagement in the Latino community, especially among immigrants, and they supported candidates who shared their progressive views on immigration reform, healthcare, and education. Many of Team Awesome's volunteers are undocumented immigrants that cannot vote. The organization registers people who can vote and educates potential Latino voters about the candidates.

In 2011, Team Awesome helped boost voter turnout by about 400 percent in West and Central Phoenix. What made the work of Team Awesome so extraordinary was the fact that so many of its volunteers were unable to vote in the very elections in which they were involved. Even as they went door to door, these young undocumented immigrants could not escape the reality that on any given day they might be deported. Deportation was more than a remote possibility; fellow DREAMers had already faced that fate. Although undocumented, DREAMer activists regarded themselves as "Americans," at least in spirit, despite not having formal legal documentation and status.

Often having arrived in the United States as small children, these young immigrants had come of age during the decade preceding the passage of SB 1070, a period that witnessed growing antagonism toward progressive policies, such as bilingual education and affirmative action, as well as a series of increasingly stringent laws aimed at deterring undocumented immigrants from coming to or remaining in Arizona. Despite their lack of legal status, undocumented immigrants by the tens of thousands graduated from high schools nationwide.

U.S. federal law required public schools to admit all students regardless of their immigration status. In Arizona, as elsewhere, these students oftentimes pursued higher education and earned degrees, even though they were legally barred from receiving federal Pell Grants and Federal student loans. Their education, however, exposed them to the U.S. civil rights struggle and, faced with growing anti-immigrant sentiment, many decided not to retreat into the shadows, but to instead stand up for their rights.

Unauthorized immigrants understood that, despite not having the right to vote, they were afforded other privileges under the U.S. Constitution, such as the right to assemble peaceably and appeal for redress in the face of injustice. While they could not be legally hired by organizations, young undocumented immigrants understood that under their constitutionally protected right to free speech they could encourage others who could do so to vote for candidates who supported policies they agreed with. While interested in and impacted by a wide array of issues, Team Awesome was most interested in working against the likes of candidates and public officials such as Pearce and in support of candidates such as 2012 Democratic candidate for U.S. Senate Richard Carmona, an impassioned supporter of the DREAM Act, a proposed law that would have allowed some undocumented immigrants to seek a path to U.S. citizenship (Alonzo 2012). While Team Awesome was publicly aligned with the Democratic Party, one volunteer, Adriana, in 2012, told *Phoenix New Times* reporter Monica Alonzo, "I don't walk for the party . . . I am walking for my community, for my family, for myself. I'm walking for my future" (2012).

Another key organization engaged in grassroots Arizona politics, particularly since the passage of SB 1070 in 2010, has been Promise Arizona (PAZ), led by long-time community organizer Petra Falcón and funded by Community Change and the Marguerite Casey Foundation. Falcón has been engaged in grassroots politics since the early days of the Chicano Movement in the 1970s. Promise Arizona's early claim to fame was a hundred-day-plus prayer vigil, led by Falcón and a group of unauthorized immigrants that began at the Arizona State Capitol on April 23, 2010. During this vigil, Promise Arizona prayed that SB 1070 would be overturned by the courts, and, like Team Awesome, Promise Arizona led far-reaching efforts to register voters and boost voter turnout, particularly among Latino voters, with the help of an army of young volunteers and undocumented immigrants. The group was a major force in the effort to recall Senator Pearce from office. Falcón has been a leading voice on immigration reform ever since. The efforts of groups such as Promise Arizona (PAZ), Team Awesome, Citizens for a Better Arizona, Unite Here, LUCHA, and Mi Familia Vota played a significant role, particularly at the grassroots level, in turning back the tide against Arizona's anti-immigrant leadership.

Coupled with the efforts of the state's business community and other community-based reactions, the response to SB 1070 helped inspire widespread opposition to draconian immigration laws passed nationwide. At the same time, it was SB 1070 that served as a catalyst for the national anti-immigrant movement of the period.

Unauthorized Mexican immigration had actually decreased dramatically prior to the passage of SB 1070, largely due to the economic slowdown in the United States and the overall improvement of the Mexican economy. Recent data show the proportion of unauthorized immigrants in Arizona had been declining since peaking in 2007. As mentioned earlier, unauthorized immigration in Arizona went down before the passage of SB 1070; it is a major misperception—one that elected officials like to perpetuate—that immigration decreased in Arizona because of tough laws like SB 1070. There are other misperceptions regarding the demographics as well. Arizona is not the state with the highest proportion of unauthorized immigrants; that would be California. In fact, proportionally, Arizona is ranked ninth in the country with unauthorized immigrants.

Furthermore, immigrant-related crime hasn't escalated. The FBI released crime statistics data illustrating that violent crime in Arizona fell nearly 14 percent in 2009—the largest drop of any state except South Dakota. Murder and non-negligent manslaughter dropped by 22 percent, and rape fell by 3.8 percent (Montini 2010). These data contradict some of the narratives by elected officials that crime was attributed to unauthorized immigrants.

Contrary to popular belief, immigrants—including unauthorized immigrants—pay taxes, create jobs, and are an overwhelming net gain to the Arizona economy (Gans 2008). Mexican immigrants also contribute to México's economy, thus reducing the pressure for additional immigration from that nation. For instance, in 2016, Mexican immigrants in the United States sent $26 billion to friends and families in México. These monies, or remittances, are the second-largest source of foreign income into México after petroleum sales, and an important part of the Mexican economy.

Some politicians have maintained that they would like to remove all unauthorized immigrants and send them back to their country of origin. A study conducted by the Center for American Progress found that it costs approximately $23,500 to apprehend, detain, and deport an immigrant. If the estimated eleven million immigrants were to be deported, it would cost $285 billion (Kasperkevic 2012).

Between 2006 and 2010, the number of immigration-related bills doubled nationally, in emulation of Arizona's SB 1070. In 2006, 570 were introduced. In 2010, the number jumped to 1,374 in just the first six months (Donnelly 2013). The wave of anti-immigrant proposals designed to decrease the unauthorized population included the denial of public benefits, emergency health care, public education, and housing. Proof of citizenship in voting and requirements for new forms of documentation were also implemented. Greater scrutiny and penalties for employers that knowingly hire unauthorized workers were also increased, though very few employers have faced prosecution. Suspension and or revocation of professional licenses if obtained by an unauthorized immigrant are being carried out in a variety of states. And there has been a substantial increase in the funding for border enforcement as well as deportation operations. Many politicians, including several Republican presidential candidates, have proposed amending the Constitution to deny citizenship to children born to undocumented parents in the United States (Donnelly 2013).

Overall, in Arizona, as a backlash to SB 1070, the state suffered several significant economic hits. The state lost $141 million in convention cancellations after SB 1070. The tourism industry lost an estimated $253 million in economic output, $9.4 million in tax revenues and 2,761 jobs (Hudson 2012).

One Arizona

In addition to this economic backlash, multiple grassroots activist organizations in opposition to SB 1070 were also founded, including One Arizona. The coalition of Latino voter-registration groups was formed in 2010 as a direct response to the growing disenfranchisement of voters and to the attack on the Latino community in the form of this "show me your papers" law. One Arizona is comprised of twenty-three organizations from all over the state, including the Arizona Center for Empowerment (ACE), Arizona Advocacy Foundation, Arizona Dream Act Coalition (ADAC), Central Arizonans for A Sustainable Economy (CASE), Chispa Arizona, Inter Tribal Council of Arizona, Mi Familia Vota, Protecting Arizona's Family Coalition, Rural Arizona Engagement (RAZE), and Puente (One Arizona n.d.). One Arizona is completely nonpartisan and focused on improving the lives of people of color and young people in Arizona through civic participation (n.d.).

Since its founding, One Arizona has grown into one of the most effective Latino advocacy organizations in the state. It has worked in a successful collaborative format on civic engagement efforts in statewide off-year and odd-year (municipal) election seasons, focusing on voter registration, voter engagement, voter mobilization, election protection, and issue advocacy. In their short existence they have been able to accomplish many important political tasks, such as enhancing interorganizational collaboration, minimizing duplication of efforts, developing best practices for data management and voter engagement, coordinating volunteer management and joint field efforts, improving evaluation measures, building rigorous accountability systems, and utilizing economies of scale to reduce costs. Their strategies focus on ensuring a strong grassroots program that meets voters where they are. Of greatest significance is the fact that they have fostered and convened a unified, coordinated front of allies and organizations focused on improving civic engagement efforts in Arizona and centered on Latinos in Arizona (One Arizona 2016b).

The executive director of One Arizona, Ian Danley, has been a powerful community organizer. The umbrella organization he created has been one of the most important immigration advocacy organizations in the state. Born and raised in west central Phoenix, over the past twelve years Danley's work has focused on issues of racial and economic justice, and immigrant students and communities. He has won numerous awards, including the César Chávez Champion of Change by the White House in 2013. Danley's projects include large-scale youth-led and volunteer-driven civic engagement campaigns that invite young people into leadership, foster a new environment of inclusive participation and develop the necessary civic infrastructure for democracy to flourish (Danley 2016).

Another prominent activist is Randy Parraz, a gifted and charismatic public speaker who cemented his reputation in Arizona politics as the head of a grassroots organization aimed at exposing the activities of the anti-immigrant extremists such as Joe Arpaio and Russell Pearce. The group, since disbanded, was called Citizens for a Better Arizona (CBA) and described by Pearce as far-left anarchists. Parraz's organization gained attention for its dogged pursuit of Arpaio by calling attention to the MCSO's alleged misdeeds and waste of taxpayer funds, though its true claim to fame came from its involvement and leadership in the 2011 recall of then–sitting Arizona Senate president Russell Pearce, at the time the state's most powerful political leader and the self-declared "president" of the state's Tea Party movement. Parraz's other leaders included Chad Snow, Paul Castañeda, and Carolyn Cooper, as well as board members Molly Durán, Fred Barlam, Saul Solis, Bob Unferth, Amanda Zill, and Mary Lou Boettcher.

In March 2015, the group shut its doors and pledged to resurface at the Arizona Blue Campaign, a fund designed to register more than two hundred thousand new Democratic voters by October 1, 2016, and help begin to lead Arizona in the Democratic aisle. In the 2014 election, a Republican won every major elected office in Arizona. In its statement, Citizens for a Better Arizona (CBA) announced that

> those that do the work of voter registration, outreach and turnout know the real cost of turning Arizona Blue is about $5 million. In short we need a budget that matches the crisis. Finally, this new mission needs to be driven by a new organization with new leaders, energy and resources to make it happen. CBA will not be that organization. However, CBA will be the first organization to contribute $100,000 to this effort and we challenge other organizations, elected officials, Democratic donors, business leaders and other individuals who share our commitment to turning Arizona Blue to match our $100,000 pledge. Our goal is to reach $1.5 million in pledges by July 1, 2015. (Lord 2015)

In one its most colorful gambits, the media-savvy CBA in 2014 brought live chickens and a man in striped prison garb to the offices of Sheriff Arpaio. The goal was to discourage Arpaio, who was dallying with the idea of running for governor, although he eventually backed the candidacy of Republican Doug Ducey, who won the race handily, thanks in part to $7 million in out-of-state funding.

In another perhaps even more colorful tactic, protesters from CBA arrived at Arpaio's offices donning Hawaiian shirts and leis intended to mock a recent trip by a sheriff's deputy, part of the department's "Cold Case Posse," which recently traveled to the island in search of evidence that President Obama was not a U.S. citizen. The group was protesting the use of $10,000 in taxpayer money spent on a nine-day stay in Hawaii. At the time, Arpaio claimed Obama's birth certificate had been doctored. No evidence for the claim has ever been provided.

During a personal discussion, Parraz provided some interesting principles and ideas for grassroots organizing strategies in Arizona (2014). First, he said that Arizona needed some new Latino leadership; there is an older generation of leaders in place that do not seem as motivated as they once were. He gave the example of Congressman Pastor, who, when SB 1070 was implemented, should have been a vocal opponent. And when his organization worked to oust Russell Pearce, established or elected Latino leaders did not help in the recall. Some leaders also complain that newer generations of activism do not appreciate the gains made by these more seasoned leaders; older Latino leaders are more concerned with their legacy or reputation in community. Focus, Parraz maintained, should be on the community.

He also said he believed that Latino leaders in Arizona need to be more in touch with grassroots organizations. He thought that grassroots organizations have a better sense of what is really going on in the community. Older Latino leaders, he said, are more concerned with their reelection. Parraz also stated that perhaps he was a better grassroots organizer because he was not an elected official: as a private citizen, he was better able to navigate Latino politics and not beholden to any electoral institution. He was also not concerned about being reelected. He said that his interest in Latino politics in Arizona began as a mission to oust Russell Pearce: the most powerful man in the State of Arizona went too far during SB 1070 when it felt like he targeted all Latinos (2014).

Talking about the recall campaign, Parraz provided some more thought-provoking insights. First, he wanted to reiterate the role of the Mormon church and how members felt that Pearce had gone too far when it came to immigration. Next, his coalition was organized to oust Pearce because of his immigration antics and not because of his party affiliation (Republican). Parraz maintained that this was why he was successfully able to get a broad group, including members from both parties: it was issue-based, not partisan. He also asserted that the DREAMers on Team Awesome provided valuable work and energy. However, he wanted to also point out that the ages on his organization varied. He said, "I had volunteers who were sixteen to seventy-nine years old" (2014).

CPLC president Edmundo Hidalgo said that it's difficult to separate the issue of immigrants' rights and civil rights in general. He maintained that immigration is so important to Latinos in Arizona, given that so many U.S.-born Latino families have relatives or recent ancestors who are immigrants. Hidalgo believed that the link between immigration and Latino politics really began in 2004, with the passage of Proposition 200, the state-approved initiative that mandates showing new forms of identification to vote. Proposition 200 had a clear message that was overtly racist and would unduly place barriers on Latinos in order to vote. He maintained that was the last time there was clear, bipartisan opposition to an immigration proposal in the state (2014).

Hidalgo maintained that Latino leaders came to that crossroads when the state passed Proposition 300 in 2006, a voter-approved referendum that barred undocumented immigrants from accessing many state taxpayer–funded services, including tuition scholarships for college and university students. This policy was too draconian. Hidalgo also said that today's DREAMers are the new Chicano Movement, that there is a real passion for change, and that he believes that one of the best assets of DREAMers is their clear message. The messaging of issue is important, and he said he feels that there are too many voices with disparate goals in Arizona Latino Politics. Hidalgo also described recent immigration attacks as "authoritarian." That is, he believes that politicians say things about immigrants that are not clearly articulated but make constituents feel safe and more American because, well, they are good messaging. Finally, CPLC did not support the boycotts as a rebuke of SB 1070: "Hurting the pocket of immigrants did not sit well with the organization" (2014).

The Puente Human Rights Movement (Puente) is a grassroots organization that focuses on migrant justice in Arizona. According to Puente's "Mission + Vision" statement, the group "aims for its participants to develop, educate, and empower migrant communities to protect and defend [their] families and [themselves]." Puente began in 2007 in response to 287(g), which granted state and local law enforcement expanded immigration enforcement power in conjunction with ICE (American Immigration Council 2020). Puente pursued several opposition campaigns, including Arrest Arpaio not the People, ICE Out of PCJ, and Alto Arizona, which was a direct response to SB 1070.

The Secure Communities (S-COMM) Program is a collaboration between local police and ICE. Under S-COMM, anyone booked into a jail can have their fingerprints checked against a database that reveals information about their immigration history. The program was enacted by the DHS to locate aliens in jails and ultimately separate criminal immigrants from others. This has resulted in immigrants not reporting illegal activity because of fear of being detained or arrested. If the police have any reason to believe an individual is undocumented, S-COMM grants permission to check fingerprints upon booking into jail; this occurs even if no charges are brought against the individual. In short, immigrants can be deported without even committing a crime.

The National Day Laborer Organizing Network (NDLON) filed a lawsuit against ICE in February 2010 to require transparency about S-COMM. Previously, the Obama administration had supported and expanded S-COMM as part of the FBI's Next Generation Identification (NGI) program, which aimed to expand the national database of biometrics for both citizens and noncitizens. *National Day Laborer Organizing Network (NDLON) v. U.S. Immigration and Customs Enforcement Agency (ICE)* was settled in July 2013 in favor of NDLON, forcing the government to release documents as to the origins of S-COMM. Puente's campaign called "Alto Arizona":

> Reassert the federal government's exclusive control over immigration law by making clear that state and local police do not have the inherent authority to enforce immigration law.
>
> Immediately suspend and terminate all police-ICE partnerships, including 287(g) agreements and the so-called "Secure Communities" initiative. Direct the Department of Homeland Security to refuse to take custody of anyone charged with violating provisions of SB 1070. (Alto Arizona n.d.)

Puente also administers the Puente Ink and Puente Vision programs, which provide space and resources for creating protest art as well as the sharing of photographic and video stories of immigrant life in the State of Arizona. Puente offers community defense courses as well, a six-week program that examines immigrant's rights and detention and deportation issues. Puente also runs a summer school for teaching children about history and art and offers a program to assist families that want to apply for DACA and DAPA status.

Carlos García, director of Puente Arizona, says:

> If there is something to "get" from the most recent resistance to the Trump effect in Arizona, it is that undocumented people are done with the era of

being beaten up on in this state. In the context of Sheriff Joe Arpaio, the wanna-be Trumps now going wild in the statehouse and the criminal justice system has been exposed as racist by the Black Lives Matter movement.

There is, in fact, no room for neutral observers. Until Arizona reverses its legacy of attrition, removes its proponents from office, and starts a process of truth and reconciliation, we are still under siege. . . .

It is to stand with those whose lives are most affected against even the slightest attack and to act on the basis that there is not one member of our community whose family is indefensible or whose human dignity is invalid. How we defend our families can be a subject of dialogue. (2016)

García, currently a council member for the City of Phoenix, remains a fierce advocate for Latinos in Maricopa County. When asked why he ran for office, he said, "We have to have our voices heard in both in the community and in the city council" (Santos et al. 2019).

Opposition to Sheriff Joe

Between 2008 and 2015, numerous protests and demonstrations were held in opposition to the activities of the MCSO. On February 6, 2009, more than seventy immigrant, labor, and civil rights organizations convened in Phoenix to protest the sheriff's forced march of shackled immigrants to a segregated area in his notorious "Tent City." The organizations condemned the sheriff's actions as a publicity stunt; they also prepared a series of teach-ins throughout the county to "increase awareness, raise funds, and energize those who wish to restore decency to the immigration reform debate" (Somos America 2009).

At a conference held in Phoenix by the local community-based organization Somos America/We Are America, the protestors' central message was to stop the sheriff's raids and revoke all 287(g) agreements. Héctor Yturralde, president of Somos America, said, "We're closing Guantanamo Bay in Cuba. Now we must stop human rights abuses here on American soil. President Obama and Secretary of Homeland Security Janet Napolitano have the power and the moral obligation to do that now by halting immigration raids and revoking all 287(g) agreements" (Somos America 2009).

Vice president of Somos America Lydia Guzmán added, "Jailing landscapers, maids and dishwashers does not make us safer. But it does tear apart families. The small children who suddenly find themselves without parents cannot wait for Congress to pass comprehensive reform. The communities being terrorized by people like Sheriff Arpaio cannot wait" (2009).

In 2009, Phoenix mayor Phil Gordon condemned Sheriff Arpaio's actions and asked attorney general Eric Holder to investigate his activities. At a César Chávez luncheon, the mayor stated, "Sheriff Joe Arpaio is locking up brown people for having broken taillights" (Lemon 2009). He also said that illegal immigration is a "race issue," and that it is a shame that this long after César Chávez we are still battling with it. The mayor criticized the Sheriff for his public relationship with and admiration for neo-Nazis: Arpaio has said that it's an honor to be called KKK and has posed for photos with high-profile neo-Nazis (Lemon 2009).

In 2012, a report found that an astounding four hundred sex crime cases between 2005 and 2007 were either inadequately investigated or ignored by the MSCO. The reason for the mishandling of these cases was simply that too much attention was placed on immigration enforcement rather than on crime reduction. Bill Louis, the police chief of El Mirage, maintained that Sheriff Arpaio moved investigators off of the sex crime cases and onto illegal immigration enforcement: "He depleted the manpower so he could further his politically motivated investigations" (Hagan 2012).

In 2012, Arpaio stated that investigations by the Justice Department and the Department of Homeland Security into the MSCO's racial profiling and mishandling of cases were simply politically motivated. At the time, Arpaio held several press conferences, stating that he had inside information on the legitimacy of President Obama's birth certificate, and that he would essentially be able to get him removed from office with his shocking insights. He said that the investigations were payback for what was going to be scandalous information about President Obama (Hagan 2012). Arpaio never released any further information. In 2012, he was once again reelected. However, his reelection was much closer than previous reelections.

Political analysts contended that if this race had not coincided with the presidential reelection as well as senate races he may not have won. Typically, voter turnout is higher in federal elections. Furthermore, Arpaio raised over $8 million for his campaign, and most of the money was from out of state. This was an extraordinary amount for a sheriff's reelection. During his acceptance speech, Arpaio vowed to develop a better relationship with the Latino community, though he also maintained that he was going to stay the course on his immigration enforcement policies.

In 2013, the grassroots nonprofit Respect Arizona launched a campaign to recall Sheriff Arpaio. Organizers fell short of the 335,000 signatures needed, and Arpaio avoided being recalled. Lilia Álvarez, campaign manager of the recall effort, "This (racial profiling) ruling would've given us a victory, really, if it would've come a month ago" (Billead 2014). Respect Arizona did not say how many signatures it eventually received. Arpaio issued a statement, saying, "This effort failed because the good people of Maricopa County, whom I'm honored to serve, rejected the wrong-headed idea of overturning an election" (2014).

In 2014, Arpaio expressed that, because of his popularity, he was considering running for state governor. He received $3.5 million in campaign donations. Interestingly, again, much of the money was from individuals who lived outside of Arizona. In June 2014, he issued a statement that he had decided not to run.

In 2015, Arpaio was taken back to federal court for contempt charges. By his own admission, Arpaio intentionally ignored the injunction by U.S. District Court Judge G. Murray Snow to stop the crime suppression sweeps and failed to direct his deputies to stop the sweeps. Also, evidence was allegedly withheld that would have shown that the MCSO had continued to racially profile Latinos despite the court orders. In a stunning turn of events, Arpaio also confessed to having the judge's wife investigated.

Deferred Action for Childhood Arrivals (DACA)

President Obama signed an executive order calling for the deferred action of unauthorized young people who came to the United States as children. Immigrants may qualify for DACA only if they meet all requirements, including (but not limited to): if the individual is not older than thirty-one as of June 15, 2012, has lived in the United States continuously for five years, came to the United States at an age younger than sixteen, and was currently in school or had graduated, among a few other residency specifications such as serving in the military. After the two-year period expires, qualified members may renew their status for another two-year period (with no apparent limitation on renewals), given that they did not violate any of the initial requirements since being approved (U.S. Congress 2018). Although some decried DACA as a political maneuver by the president to gain more Latino support in the 2012 election, it is still in effect today. Under DACA, qualified individuals may be exempt from deportation for a period of two years and are authorized to legally attain employment. DACA guarantees that the youth will not be deported and provides a temporary work permit for two years. Approximately a hundred million individuals qualified for DACA as of 2017, and approximately seven hundred thousand had applied.

The program was informally intended to eliminate the threat of deportation for children who illegally immigrated to the United States without any choice (i.e., were brought by their parents at a young age); it has the added bonus of keeping educated immigrants in the United States to benefit the economy. Although most of the approved applicants in Arizona are of Mexican heritage, DACA has provided benefits to thousands of immigrants from at least twenty countries. In Arizona, specifically, about thirty thousand applicants have been approved.

According to the American Immigration Council, 59 percent of "DREAMers" (the informal title given approved applicants of the program) obtained a new job and 45 percent increased job earnings with benefits available under DACA. 21 percent of DREAMers were able to attain health care. 86 percent have worked for pay, 67 percent were employed at the time of the survey, and 34 percent had more than one job. The findings suggest that the population of immigrants eligible for DACA can greatly add to the economy in terms of income and high-skill jobs (2013).

In Arizona, two of the most prominent controversies for DREAMers concern eligibility for in-state tuition and the ability to obtain a driver's license. According to a 2006 state referendum, Proposition 300, people without lawful immigration status are not eligible for in-state tuition. On this basis, then–attorney general Tom Horne sued the Maricopa County College District in Phoenix in 2013 for permitting DREAMers to pay in-state tuition. He told reporters that his views on the law are irrelevant, and his job is to enforce the law. Multiple attempts by advocates to persuade Horne to drop the lawsuit were unsuccessful. In October 2013, a group of activists met with Horne to request that the suit be dropped; the meeting turned into a dispute about the attorney general's own misdemeanors and legal run-ins. One Maricopa College faculty member claimed that DREAMers being removed from her classroom resembled Nazi Germany, and Horne only argued with her about the plausibility of that comparison. That group left after the general consensus was that Horne would not be changing his mind about the lawsuit.

A week later, activist Randy Parraz of Citizens for a Better Arizona directed a demonstration outside of Horne's office. DREAMers burned copies of their high school diplomas to signify the uselessness of their education without access to affordable higher education. According to *Phoenix New Times* writer Ray Stern, four of the DREAMers, dressed in full graduation attire, even attempted to deliver Horne a burrito from a food truck, "hoping to symbolize their potential future without a degree" (2013).

Mark Brnovich, who replaced Horne, decided to keep Horne's initial lawsuit going. Congress members Raúl Grijalva, Ann Kirkpatrick, and Ruben Gallego wrote to Brnovich to request that he drop the lawsuit, maintaining that the USCIS believes that DACA beneficiaries are lawfully present. Brnovich replied that the agency does not confer lawful status upon an individual.

Judge Arthur Anderson of the Maricopa County Superior Court ruled in May 2015 that federal law does not determine that person's lawful presence. Two days after Judge Anderson's ruling, the Arizona state Board of Regents announced that in-state tuition would be available to DREAMers in public and community colleges universities.

After Judge Anderson's ruling, President Obama took executive action to expand DACA to include all immigrants who are either in school or have graduated, who entered the United States as children, and who have a clean criminal record. He also created a sister program called Deferred Action for Parents of Americans and Lawful Permanent Residents (DAPA), which would restrict deportation for parents of DREAMers as well. A federal judge issued a temporary injunction as twenty-six states, including Arizona, sued the federal government to block the new programs.

The difference between in-state and out-of-state tuition is substantial enough to warrant the years of legal battles. The Maricopa County Community Colleges charge $84 per credit for in-state residents and $325 per credit for students without Arizona residency. Likewise, the University of Arizona charges $11,000 for in-state tuition, but $29,500 for non-Arizona residents. Over a typical four-year undergraduate experience, that amounts to a $74,000 difference.

Another of the main struggles facing DREAMers in Arizona was Governor Brewer's declaration that DACA employment authorization does not constitute sufficient evidence for legal status, and thus that DREAMers cannot attain Arizona driver's licenses. Brewer issued the executive order in August 2012, claiming that Obama's DACA does not confer lawful or authorized status.

In November 2012, the Arizona Dream Act Coalition filed a class action lawsuit against Brewer, saying her executive order overstepped the federal government's power, violating the Supremacy and Equal Protection Clauses. In *Arizona Dream Act v. Janice K. Brewer*, the U.S. Supreme Court ordered Arizona to end the ban on driver's licenses in December 2014, and, in January 2015, Judge David Campbell of the Arizona U.S. District Court sided with ADAC. According to Judge Campbell, Brewer and the defendants "argue that DACA recipients are not similarly situated because their authorization to stay—unlike the authorization of other EAD holders who may obtain a driver's license—is the result of prosecutorial discretion." He continued: "The Court does not agree. DACA recipients have been authorized by the federal government to remain in the United States for two years and have been granted the right to work through the issuance of EADs. Other noncitizens are in similar positions." Because Brewer and her attorneys could not prove that DACA's authorization of employment is different from other federal authorizations, and the basis of her argument was that DACA gives different benefits than other programs, the court ruled in favor of the plaintiffs. The number of Arizona DREAMers will expand if the courts decide to allow President Obama's expansion of DACA and implementation of DAPA.

Proposition 300 was passed in 2006. The law denies a student in-state tuition even if they have lived in Arizona for decades. If the student is unauthorized, they are also ineligible for any tuition assistance. The Arizona Dream

Act Coalition (ADAC) was founded by a group of undocumented students from ASU opposing Prop. 300. Since its founding, ADAC has been involved with a number of programs and campaigns throughout Arizona. The organization has facilitated civic engagement campaigns over the last few years. In 2011 and 2014, ADAC provided education and outreach regarding voting and assisting with registering citizens to vote. Incredibly, ADAC members cannot vote, yet they are providing outreach on the process.

Ellie

Many remarkable DACA activists attend ASU. In a course entitled Arizona, Immigration, Latinos and Politics, students are asked to share their story: who they are and how they got to where they are today. Many of these stories are impressive and humbling. Ellie's, however, is one of the most memorable (Pérez 2016). She provided permission to share her story for this book.

Ellie Pérez remembers crawling under a tin-like fence, her father pulling her into his arms while reaching for her older sister. Her mother was carrying her baby sister in her arms. She remembers her parents dusting her off and quickly rushing the family into an old, beige-colored, two-door Mercury Grand Marquis. Her uncle, who had driven down to the Nogales border, drove them to their new home in Phoenix, Arizona. Ellie was four years old. She says that to this day she can still see that car waiting for them on the other side.

Ellie arrived in Phoenix on September 24, 1995. Her parents brought her and her two sisters from Xalapa, Veracruz, México, to be reunited with relatives in Phoenix, Arizona. Her dad said he wanted a better life and future for the family.

She grew up attending public schools and says that she picked up a love for learning. Her family was poor, but Ellie says that her mom made sure that they received a good education. Ellie attended the Paradise Valley School District, and she says that teachers were a big part of who she is today. Growing up, her teachers told her she could do anything and everything she wanted to do.

Ellie says she never really understood her legal status in this country. It was not until she was a high school sophomore at the age of sixteen that she saw friends getting driver's licenses and, more important, their first jobs. She says, "I applied everywhere, but never got any jobs. I was regularly asked if I was sure my information was correct. It was then that I understood that even though I had grown up in the United States and was as American as anyone else, I wasn't legal" (Pérez 2016). Although she had done the hard work to prepare herself for college and she had exceptional grades, it would not be an option.

In May 2009, she became the first high school graduate in her family. She recalls her mother and sisters watching her receive her diploma with tears in their eyes. Ellie says she had no idea how she was going to afford college, but her mother found her a job, working with her. For an entire year, she worked with her mother cleaning all day, every day.

In July 2010, she had enough money to pay for her first semester at Paradise Valley Community College. Unauthorized students had to pay out-of-state tuition, so it was quite expensive. By the fall of that year, Ellie was a college freshman. She continued to work and save enough money to take one or two classes each semester.

The same year she started community college, in 2010, she had to decide if she was going to stay in Phoenix and continue school or leave the country and go back to México with her mother, despite having lived in the United States for fifteen years. The family was afraid of staying in Arizona because of SB 1070. Ellie says she feels lucky because her mom and sisters decided to stay in Arizona and see what happened: "The effects of SB 1070 had caused so much fear in my community, and soon, friends and family members were leaving the state. The first year that law was in effect was honestly pretty scary. The very real fact that if my mom was pulled over while driving, and we were not in the car with her, she could be arrested and taken back to México, was more terrifying than anything" (Pérez 2016).

In 2012, President Obama announced that he would, as part of an executive decision, grant deferred action to students like Ellie. She would be able to legally work in the country for at least two years, but, more important, attend school without fear.

In that same year, she came upon a group of young students who, like her, were undocumented, and were known as Team Awesome. They introduced her to political organizing. Ellie says she "immediately fell in love" with organizing (2016). She notes that these students had taken it upon themselves to change their lives by mobilizing every Latino that could legally vote in Phoenix. They also worked to elect leaders who believed in DREAMers and would fight to protect them and their families.

Ellie became one of the lead volunteers for Kyrsten Sinema's congressional campaign. Congresswoman Sinema was elected, and Ellie felt that her team was a small part of that victory. After her first political campaign, she says, there was no going back: she could legally work in this country and had found her passion. In January 2013, she volunteered for Kate Gallego's city council campaign in Phoenix. Gallego won that race and was on the city council from 2014 to 2018. Ellie said, "In those two years, I had not only fallen in love with organizing, but I had empowered my community. That feeling outweighed the fear I had once felt" (2016). In 2019 Gallego became the mayor of Phoenix.

In 2015, Ellie received her associate degree, becoming the first in her family. Moreover, she was accepted to ASU: her first choice. Fortunately, months before starting ASU, the Board of Regents granted DACA students in-state tuition, drastically reducing the costs to attend college.

Unforgettably, when Ellie told her story to the class, she concluded with tears in her eyes: "If there is anyone in this class that can vote and doesn't, don't talk to me because you don't know how lucky you are" (2016).

Councilwoman Gallego offered Ellie a position on her city council office staff. Ellie is the first DREAMer to ever work and serve the City of Phoenix. Her job is to mobilize and advocate for Latino immigrants. Ellie later worked on Hillary Clinton's campaign. She continues to work with Democratic National Committee chair Tom Pérez. At the presidential address in Washington, D.C., in 2019, Ellie was the guest of Congressman Gordon. She is one of the most prominent activists in Arizona.

In the lawsuit *Arizona Dream Act Coalition v. Brewer*, ADAC challenged legislation that denied the effects of Deferred Action for Childhood Arrivals (DACA). Under DACA, undocumented children that meet a certain list of requirements can remain in Arizona without fear of deportation. Legislation supported by Governor Brewer, including Executive Order 2012–06, would have denied all children eligible for DACA any "state identification, including a driver's license." The courts sided with ADAC, instructing the courts to enter a preliminary injunction to prohibit issuance of state identification on grounds of requiring proof of work.

In addition to civic engagement, ADAC focuses on creating educational opportunities for both high school students and graduates. High school students have expanded access to information about postsecondary institutions and scholarships while graduates have options for professional development (e.g., résumé workshops, job searches). Another of ADAC's programs includes Education Not Deportation (END). The goal was originally to stop deportation of students-DREAMers, but, because it was so successful, its expanded aim has shifted to non-DREAMer students.

CHAPTER 4

Latino Political Strategies

I n the 2008 presidential election, Arizona ranked twenty-ninth in terms of its total share of Latinos who were eligible to vote in the national election, making up approximately 673,000 individuals, or 17 percent of the total eligible voters in Arizona (Pew Research Center 2008). Election-day exit polls nationwide found that Barack Obama won 67 percent of the Latino vote, while John McCain received 32 percent. This represented a 5-percent decrease compared to 2004, when approximately 37 percent of Latino voters supported George W. Bush.

In Arizona, McCain lost the Latino vote to Obama 56 percent to 41 percent. The exit polls in Arizona revealed that the policy concerns of Latinos were similar to those of non-Latinos, but immigration was very important. Arizona, in 2008, perhaps owing to the fact that it was not considered a competitive state, saw its turnout rate below the national average. Approximately 32 percent of Arizona's voting age population voted, while the national average was 37.

Another possible explanation for the low 2008 voter turnout can be extrapolated by looking at the characteristics of a large segment of Latino eligible voters. Demographically, 32 percent of all Latino eligible voters in Arizona were ages eighteen to twenty-nine and more likely to be native-born citizens (81 percent). Olivier Richomme (2017) affirms that "this has important electoral consequences since young people register and turn out at much lower rates than older people." Further, in terms of education, 28 percent of Latino eligible voters in Arizona did not complete high school—more than double the percentage (13 percent) of all eligible voters in Arizona. Historically, voter turnout rates have depended on a multitude of demographic variables, with education attainment and age being two of the key predictors (2017).

In 2008, McCain's vacillating position on immigration exemplifies the difficulty GOP candidates encounter both in Arizona and nationwide soliciting Latino votes while placating their party's far-right wing. In 2005 and 2007, McCain supported a comprehensive, bipartisan immigration reform bill. In 2008, when he ran for president, he received harsh criticism from the Republican right for supporting any comprehensive immigration reform (Tobar 2016). In fact, when addressing these critics, he said he would no longer support his own previous stance on immigration. In 2010, while running for reelection to the U.S. Senate, McCain again reversed his stance on immigration reform. His reelection was in the same year that SB 1070 passed. He ran against a hard-right conservative, J. D. Hayworth. Indicative of his shifting stance on immigration, McCain ran a commercial that said, "Let's finish the dang fence," even though he had previously been an ardent opponent of building a wall between the United States and México (after his reelection, in 2013, McCain rechampioned another comprehensive, moderate immigration reform proposal).

In the 2012 presidential election, 71 percent of Latinos nationwide voted for President Obama and 27 percent voted for Mitt Romney. This was the highest show of Latino support for a president since 1996, when the candidate was Bill Clinton. The 2012 election also had the highest number of Latinos that turned out to vote overall, accounting for 10 percent of total voter turnout nationally, as compared to 2008, when Latinos accounted for 9 percent in the presidential election. Florida, Colorado, and Nevada, with their large Latino populations, are key presidential campaign battleground states. President Obama easily won the Latino vote in all three.

In 2014, the Latino vote had a significant influence on some key races, such as for seats in the Senate and Congress—for example, on two congressional seats in Arizona. District 1 contained approximately 105,000 Latino eligible voters, and District 2 85,000. Arizona has two Latinos in the House of Representatives: Ruben Gallego of Phoenix and Raúl Grijalva of Tucson. Congressman Ed Pastor previously held Gallego's position before his retirement in 2014. Indicative of the growing importance of the Latino vote, Scott Fistler, previously a Republican, changed his name to César Chávez for election purposes. His motivation for the name change, he stated, was that he wanted to be recognizable to Latinos (Sánchez 2014).

Partisan politics have been contentious when it comes to Latinos and immigration. In 2012, after his presidential defeat, Mitt Romney said that one of his regrets was not targeting the Latino community and not providing a better explanation of the Republican position on immigration. Only 15 percent of Latino voters in the United States identified with the Republican Party at the time (Pew Research Center 2013).

After the 2012 election, moderate Republicans tried to come up with a plan to boost Latino political participation in upcoming races. When Mitt Romney ran for president in 2012, 89 percent of his voters were white. The Republican National Committee (RNC) chair Reince Priebus called for a series of focus groups to determine how they could better target nonwhite voters (Dickson 2013). The resulting data was used to create the "growth and opportunity project" report (Woodruff 2016). This self-critique—or "Republican autopsy"—allowed the RNC to come up with a plan to encourage greater Latino participation in the Republican Party:

It is imperative that the RNC changes how it engages with Hispanic communities to welcome in new members of our Party. If Hispanic Americans hear that the GOP doesn't want them in the United States, they won't pay attention to our next sentence. . . . If Hispanics think that we do not want them here, they will close their ears to our policies. . . . Hispanic voters tell us our Party's position on immigration has become a litmus test, measuring whether we are meeting them with a welcome mat or a closed door. Throughout our discussions with various Hispanic groups, they told us this: Message matters. Too often Republican elected officials spoke about issues important to the Hispanic community using a tone that undermined the GOP brand within Hispanic communities. Repairing that relationship will require both a tone that "welcomes in" as well as substantial time spent in the community demonstrating a commitment to addressing its unique concerns. As one participant in a regional listening session noted, "The key problem is that the Republican Party's message offends too many people unnecessarily." . . . As one conservative, Tea-Party leader, Dick Armey, told us, "You can't call someone ugly and expect them to go to the prom with you." (Reifowitz 2015)

It appears that the RNC did not follow its own advice. In 2013, the "Gang of Eight"—a group of eight senators, four Republicans and four Democrats—created a comprehensive immigration proposal, its major objective providing a path to citizenship, whereby nearly eleven million unauthorized immigrants could become citizens. The legalization portion of this bill would not be implemented until the DHS provided a strategy of greater border protection. The bill also sponsored a modified DREAM Act, which provides those with an education or military service and a clean background an opportunity to become citizens. Furthermore, it offers additional green-card opportunities to agricultural workers who have spent a certain amount of time in the United States.

The bill also substantially changed the structure of the immigration process. It provided more categories for "immediate family members," making more people eligible to receive a green card. The system would be merit-based and would weigh the candidate's history and skills. The bill also promoted greater enforcement and protection at the border while increasing penalties for smuggling.

This bill passed the Senate and seemed destined to go to the White House for President Obama's signature. However, Tea Party Republicans became outraged that the bill supported legalization and a path to citizenship. Many in their ranks decided to fight against the bill and not allow it to come up for a vote in Congress. Some of these members favored a piecemeal approach to immigration reform rather than one comprehensive bill—for example, Marco Rubio, one of the original members of the Gang of Eight. He wrote the bill, but, after much opposition by the far right, he then actively fought against its passage only a few months later.

Following this outcry from some Republicans in the House, the issue of comprehensive immigration reform remains uncertain. Marco Rubio is not alone: other Republicans that ran for president and have also recanted their support for immigration reform include New Jersey governor Chris Christie,

Wisconsin governor Scott Walker, Texas's junior U.S. senator Ted Cruz, and president Donald Trump. Being a moderate Republican when it came to immigration was not politically advantageous in the 2016 presidential climate. Some argue that opposition to a bipartisan bill on immigration stems from the fear that allowing millions of people to naturalize will ultimately mean that those—mostly Latino—people will vote as Democrats. While most Latinos do lean Democratic, the biggest problem facing Republican leadership is how to court the Latino vote.

Arizona is routinely described as "ground zero" on the immigration debate. Several of the Republican candidates visited Arizona while highlighting immigration concerns. The Republican candidates showed that they would be tough on immigration, as Arizona was with SB 1070. For instance,

> it turns out that Donald Trump was just warming up when he said of Mexican immigrants, 'They're bringing drugs. They're bringing crime. They're rapists.' He's not just doubling down. He's tripling down, quadrupling down. . . . what Trump knew instinctively—or perhaps what Trump knew by studying recent Arizona history–is that when it comes to anti-immigrant politics the facts . . . Do. Not. Matter.
>
> It's about perception. It's about politics. Trump really *is* mimicking on a national scale what Sheriff Joe Arpaio and former state Sen. Russell Pearce were saying in Arizona a couple of years ago. And for a while it worked great. It got all kinds of state and local politicians elected, including former Gov. Jan Brewer. (Montini 2015)

At a rally in Phoenix, Trump supporters violently ripped anti-Trump placards from the hands of protesters. Candidates made the calculation that they should maintain outreach with their base that does not support immigration reform. In February 2016, *Washington Post* and Univision found that 80 percent of Latinos had an "unfavorable view of Mr. Trump," and of this 80 percent 72 percent had a "very unfavorable view." Trump was the most disliked of all the Republican candidates in this survey (Balz and Clement 2016).

During the Arizona primary, Trump received political endorsements from both former Maricopa County sheriff Joe Arpaio and former governor Jan Brewer. Trump stated that he had the endorsement of the toughest sheriff in America, illustrating that he was the harshest of all the presidential candidates when it comes to immigration. The optics of these endorsements would play well nationally. The weekend prior to the primary election, Donald Trump came to Arizona, when national attention was focused once again on Latinos and immigration. Not surprisingly, many of the organizations that opposed Trump's visit were some of the same ones that sprouted from their opposition to SB 1070. For instance, the organization Puente made national news when three of their members were arrested for protesting Trump's visit.

When Doug Ducey successfully ran for governor in 2015, he too wanted the endorsements of Governor Brewer and Sheriff Arpaio. However, since Arpaio had been charged with racially profiling Latinos in Phoenix and was sentenced to prison for contempt of court, the governor's support was noticeably absent. In March 2016, Trump won the Arizona presidential primary. He did have the endorsements of Arpaio and Brewer, but he did not have an endorsement from Arizona's current governor, Doug Ducey. It appears that the lessons from SB 1070 and Arizona's ever-emerging Latino voting bloc and new Latino politics have somewhat tempered sitting politicians from pursuing overtly anti-immigrant agendas. In 2016, two other anti-immigration bills were introduced. Some of the same arguments were made by the Phoenix Chamber of Commerce stating that there would be economic blowback if either of the proposed legislations passed. These bills never made it to Governor Ducey to sign.

In 2016, the Democratic presidential candidate Hillary Clinton came out forcefully in support of immigration reform. Her stance exceeded previous recommendations. Indicative of her strong message was her naming Lorella Praeli, a DREAMer and a vocal advocate for immigration, as her campaign's Latino outreach director. Clinton's choice "also [sent] a message to Republican candidates to take a clearer position on immigration—a contentious issue for the GOP—as they court Latino votes. Clinton said she supported full and equal citizenship for unauthorized immigrants, saying that anything less is code for second-class status" (Lilley 2015).

At the time of Trump's presidential candidacy, political strategists both Democratic and Republican revealed that surrounding beliefs regarding the vote in Arizona indicated that it could go to either candidate. Traditionally, Arizona is a Republican state, but its physical position within the border region of México and the United States, as well as its steadily growing Latino population, created contrasting views of Trump and his candidacy. Some Arizonans strongly supported Trump and his ideology, yet, due to the changing demographics of the state, a large part of the population had a strong negative reaction toward him. From the beginning of his campaign, Trump's rhetoric that immigrants (at its core, people of Mexican origin) were "criminals and rapists" set the stage for his campaign and aimed to inspire fear within Americans who were already uneasy about the U.S. Latino population.

Additionally, Trump used his celebrity status from years of reality television as a platform to appeal emotionally to the nation at his raucous and increasingly popular rallies. One of Trump's strategies was to employ musical language and theater to strengthen his grandiose persona. Through this type of "show," Trump was able to present himself as "epic" and a "savior" here to save the oppressed peoples from the political elites (Graber 2017). Furthermore, his speeches consisted of exaggerated, mocking gestures delivered both to entertain his audience and to present himself as dominant. Through these shows, he represented himself as a self-made businessman and rescuer who held the best interests of the working class (Graber 2017).

The Trump campaign also fed on the nostalgia of the working class via his use of the campaign slogan "Make America Great Again." An offshoot of President Reagan's slogan in the 1980s, and earlier utilized by presidential rival and fellow candidate Ted Cruz during the 2016 primary, "Make America Great Again" spoke loudly to white, blue-collar workers across the nation and tugged most effectively on the heartstrings of the non–college-educated whites that believed their existence to be under threat by other racial groups, which is a decades-long Republican trend: turning ethnic minorities into scapegoats for problems that concern the average white, blue-collar worker, and, in Trump's case, the problems affecting the contemporary United States.

The "Make America Great Again" slogan promoted the idea that economic and cultural security had been greater at an earlier time in history, when America was less diverse, further reinforcing Trump's most consistent policy stance: hostility toward people of color residing in the United States (Tarenopolsky 2017). The campaign's racial rhetoric—attacking people of Mexican origin, immigrants, women, and Muslims—was an important strategic move that would unite the American white working class to Trump's advantage and, in effect, normalize taboo racist behaviors (Hoffer 2017). Although his campaign's accusations against people of color were not based on facts, Trump was able to create a narrative that brought him voters based on proposals like banning travel to the United States from countries with large Muslim populations and building a wall to prevent immigrants from entering.

In Arizona, Trump's message and campaign rhetoric lost him some support. The *Arizona Republic*, a long-standing newspaper that was once called the *Arizona Republican*, refused to endorse him and instead endorsed Hillary Clinton—the first time in 130 years that this traditionally conservative paper endorsed a candidate from the Democratic Party. As the editorial board explained its reasoning,

> Trump responds to criticism with the petulance of verbal spit wads. "That's beneath our national dignity," and in favor of Clinton, "She does not casually say things that embolden our adversaries and frighten our allies. Her approach to governance is mature, confident and rational." . . . Since the *Arizona Republic* began publication in 1890, we have never endorsed a Democrat over a Republican for president. Never. This reflects a deep philosophical appreciation for conservative ideals and Republican principles. This year is different. The 2016 Republican candidate is not conservative, and he is not qualified. That's why, for the first time in our history, The Arizona Republic will support a Democrat for president. (Mettler 2019)

Trump also lost support from Arizona state representatives and fellow Republicans such as senators John McCain and Jeff Flake, both of whom vocally expressed their disagreement with and disapproval of Trump's sexist and racially charged statements. McCain went so far as to make a statement that he and his wife would not be voting for Trump, due to his sexist comments. Flake went even further, declaring that Trump should withdraw from the race. Flake continued to hold his position to not support Trump while McCain changed his rhetoric and stance and decided that he needed to endorse Trump in order to keep his own elected position. Other Republicans, like Yavapai County attorney Sheila Polk, who was among the first to rescind support, also voiced her distaste for Trump and his xenophobic rhetoric.

Despite this opposition, others in Arizona continued to support Trump's discourse. Key leaders in the state such as Jan Brewer, Joe Arpaio, and Doug Ducey spoke openly about their support of Trump and his tough stance on immigration. In a statement of support, Brewer shared the following:

> Mr. Trump will secure our borders, defend our workers and protect our sovereignty. Mr. Trump will stand for our law enforcement, our police and our immigration officers. Mr. Trump will actually enforce the rule of law. This may be our last chance to ensure our children grow up in a country with borders, and with a government that protects its own people. This is our chance— Donald Trump is our chance—to save this country and Make America Great Again. (Scott 2016)

In a similar fashion, Arpaio, who was known for his harsh treatment of unauthorized persons and Latinos, publicly supported Trump and his proposed anti-immigration policies.

To gain more support along his campaign trail, Trump visited Arizona on numerous occasions. In March 2016, a rally supporting Donald Trump and Joe Arpaio was held in Fountain Hills, where protestors succeeded in delaying the event by obstructing access to the venue for about an hour: in one area, about two dozen cars blocked the highway to stop drivers on their way to the rally (Rosen 2016). Closer to the venue, cars and protestors holding signs saying "Comb Over Racism: Dump Trump," "Shut Down Trump," and "Stand Against Racism" blocked traffic on the major road leading to Fountain Park (Johnson et al. 2016). The protests were seen by many as an exercise of their right to demonstration; conversely, Governor Ducey believed their actions to be out of line. Within a couple of months, he signed a measure into law that increased penalties on protesters who block traffic to political events (Rosen 2016).

Arizona has a history of voter suppression. The state has been monitored for violating provisions of the Voting Rights Act, such as making it more difficult to vote or requesting more than usual documentation in order to vote. For instance, for the 2012 primaries in Maricopa County, voting locations were reduced from two hundred to sixty before the primaries (O'Dell et al. 2016); importantly, this county has approximately a 30-percent Latino population. In South Phoenix, where the population is predominantly Latino, approximately 62.5 percent, only one polling location was available, causing long lines and wait times in order to cast a ballot (Gray 2013). Similarly, West Phoenix, whose population is also predominantly Latino, had zero polling stations available. By contrast, affluent areas of Maricopa county, with its multiple polling locations, reported shorter lines and wait times.

Prior to the 2016 presidential primary election, out of the 992,000 eligible Latinos in Arizona, 470,374 Latinos were registered to vote statewide. Among these registered Latino voters, the party registration breakdown was as follows: Democratic—209,170 (44 percent); Republican—68,063 (15 percent); and Other—193,141 (41 percent).

TABLE 5 Party representation in Arizona, population: 7.28 million (Latino: 2.1 million)

Party name	Registered	Percent (%)
Republican	1,363,935	34.7%
Independent	1,301,292	33.14%
Democrat	1,228,745	31.29%
Libertarian	32,677	0.83%
Total:	3,926,649	

Source: State of Arizona Registration Report, January 2, 2020, https://azsos.gov/sites /default/files/2020_0121_January_State_Voter_Registration.pdf.

TABLE 6 Arizona general voter turnout (2008–2018)

Year	Turnout percent
2008	77.69%
2010	55.65%
2012	74.36%
2014	47.52%
2016	74.17%
2018	64.85%
2020	Exceeded 2016

Source: "Voter Registration and Historical Election Data," Arizona Secretary of State, https://azsos.gov/elections/voter-registration-historical-election-data (accessed November 16, 2020).

TABLE 7 Number of Latinos voting in recent elections in Arizona

Year	Number of Latino voters
2008	291,000
2012	400,000
2016	550,000 (89% increase in 8 years)

Source: Nancy LeTourneau, "Gauging the Latino Vote in Arizona, Nevada, and Texas," *Washington Monthly*, October 15, 2018, https://washingtonmonthly.com/2018/10/15 /gauging-the-latino-vote-in-arizona-nevada-and-texas/.

ELIGIBLE LATINO VOTERS IN ARIZONA, 2020

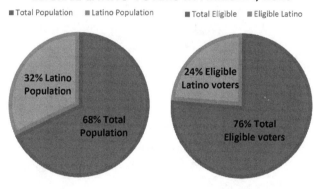

FIGURE 2 Eligible Latino voters in Arizona, 2020.

LATINO PARTY AFFILIATION IN 2018

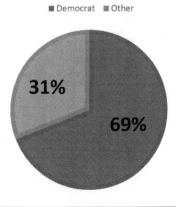

FIGURE 3 Latino party affiliations in 2018.

Grassroots collaborative community organization One Arizona formed in 2010 in response to the passing of SB 1070. The organization aimed to increase the Latino vote in Arizona and did so by promoting full electoral participation of the Latino electorate. One Arizona has since continued to educate and empower Arizonans of Latino origin while evolving with the political climate to now also target "New American Majority" (NAM) voters, made up of citizens aged eighteen to thirty and people of color (e.g., Asians, African Americans, Middle Easterners), LGBTQ individuals, unmarried women, and millennials (Robles 2017). This group is called the New American Majority because this population has seen large increases in nontraditional voters in the last local, state, and national-level elections. In the near future, unmarried women, Latinos, and other people of color will be the dominant majority (2017). It is this segment of voters that One Arizona and their collaborating community organizations focus on in an effort to educate and increase their turnout through voter registration, voter mobilization, and election protection.

During the 2016 campaigns, many political pundits stated that Arizona could possibly become a blue state and that Democratic nominee Hillary Clinton could win Arizona if the state's Latino population were to turn out at above average rates to the voting polls. Even GOP strategists were anticipating a large Latino turnout (Rucker 2016). Democrats believed that Trump's campaign would galvanize a new generation of Latino voters who had not participated in the elections before. According to Avinash Iragavarapu, executive director of the Arizona Republican Party headquarters in Phoenix during the 2016 campaign, the GOP had a 200,000-person advantage in voter registration, and, historically, voter turnout was in favor of the Republican party, as was the case in 2012, when Mitt Romney defeated Obama in the state (Rucker 2016).

In 2016, it was thought that Trump's anti-Latino rhetoric would stimulate a new era of Latino voters in Arizona. Latinos who made up about 30 percent of the state's population in 2016, but only 18 percent of the Arizona electorate in the 2012 presidential election, were a focal point for One Arizona and their collaborative partner organizations. It was thought that the estimated 350,000 Latinos who were not registered to vote in 2012 could easily be persuaded to join in 2016, due to the effect that a Trump election would have on their community. Francisco Heredia, national field director of Mi Familia Vota, a Phoenix-based Latino civic engagement organization, believed Trump to be a major motivator to the Latino community to come out and vote (Rucker 2016). And Pita Juárez of One Arizona stated, "Latinos want to vote this year. We're seeing that across the state" (2016). This was evidenced by their ability to register 120,000 voters before the November 2016 election: 40,000 more voters than their goal of 80,000. In the past, Democrats have not been successful in mobilizing Latino voters, although their demographic numbers continue to rise, but Trump's negative and divisive rhetoric apparently galvanized this community, which saw a large increase in the number of citizenship applications and voter registration among Latinos.

In addition to this surge, and in response to the Trump campaign's anti-Latino rhetoric and strong anti-immigration stance, undocumented youth also became key motivators of the Latino vote increase. With their movement, they took part in the political process by speaking out about their experiences and pleading for an increase in Latino voter turnout. One young man stated, "I can't vote, but I'm making sure all my cousins and my friends are voting for someone who's going to give me a better tomorrow. So, I think my vote just multiplied by five, by ten, whatever it is" (Mendoza 2016). Unauthorized workers had also joined in raising awareness to vote by pushing their family members and friends to use their legal status to increase their electoral power.

Although Trump won the election, these organizational efforts have created a strong, organized, and growing political movement. According to Eric Hershberg, director of the Center for Latin American and Latino Studies at American University in Washington, "In a place like Arizona, and I would add elsewhere, substantial success in efforts to promote Latino turnout could lead to a remarkable outcome" (Mendoza 2016).

The 2016 election in Arizona—specifically, in Maricopa County—brought about significant election-day victories for the Democratic party that greatly impacted the state and county's Latino populace. During the 2016 election, Joe Arpaio was defeated by the Democratic challenger Paul Penzone, and Proposition 206 ("Fight for 15"), a historic minimum wage increase, was voted into law.

In November 2016, Sheriff Arpaio, who became a national figure by cracking down on illegal immigration and forcing jail inmates to wear pink underwear while living in outdoor "tent cities," lost after a quarter-century of service, 54.9 percent to 45.1 percent to Paul Penzone, a Democrat and former Phoenix police sergeant (Santos 2016). Several important factors contributed to Arpaio's defeat: his steady decline in support from 2000 until 2016; the changing demographics of Maricopa County; voter mobilization efforts hosted by advocacy organizations; and, lastly, Arpaio's legal problems, which led to criminal charges shortly before the 2016 election.

A pattern of declining support for Arpaio had been observable in elections since 2000 and nearly reached a tipping point in 2012, when he was only able to win by 6 points against Paul Penzone. This was a stark contrast to the results in 2000, when he easily won reelection with 66.5 percent of the total vote. Arpaio's gradually declining support could be attributed to the intense local and national backlash and criticism over his illegal tactics to enforce immigration and continued legal woes regarding his possible racial profiling of Latinos, as evidenced by the following: 1992: 57.6 percent; 1996: uncontested; 2000: 66.5 percent; 2004: 56.7 percent; 2008: 55.1 percent; 2012: 50.7 percent; and 2016: 45.1 percent (Wyloge 2012). The decrease could be seen throughout the county; in the urban Phoenix area, the center of the county, Arpaio only received around 20 percent of the vote. On the other hand, rural areas gave him more than 70 percent of their vote (2012).

Another important aspect of his decrease in popularity and his 2016 election loss can be linked to the steadily changing demographics of Maricopa County over the years. According to the *Arizona Republic*, since 2010 Maricopa County has taken in approximately "148,000 people from other states and 53,000 from other countries" (2018). According to One Arizona, due to the growth in Arizona's Latino population, the number of Latino eligible voters in the state grew from 796,000 in 2008 to 1.1 million in 2016 (2018). By 2016, Latinos made up approximately 30 percent of Arizona's total population, and about 20 percent of all registered voters in the state (2018). The majority of the state's Latino population resides within Maricopa County: "About 60% of all Arizona's Hispanics live in Maricopa County, home to the fifth-largest Latino population of any county in the U.S" (Jordan 2016). Due to these changes in the racial/ethnic makeup of Arizona's population, and the

Latino and Latino-supporting community's backlash over Joe Arpaio's immigration enforcement tactics, Arpaio did not carry areas with more registered Republicans than Democrats in the 2016 election, such as Ahwatukee, Tempe, Chandler, west Mesa, Paradise Valley, northeast Phoenix, south Scottsdale, and some isolated precincts in Glendale and Peoria (Wyloge 2012).

Latino voter mobilization efforts driven by Latino-driven advocacy groups such as Bazta Arpaio, Puente, and One Arizona also greatly contributed to the defeat of Joe Arpaio in the 2016 election: "Latinos, who have been battling him for years, made a significant contribution to Arpaio's defeat" (Jordan 2016). The combination of the changing Maricopa County demographics and the work of local grassroots organizations that aimed to increase the minority vote led to more than 100,000 new voters for the 2016 election: "America's Toughest Sheriff's defeat is the result of many campaigns and protests led mostly by Latino activists. It means Latinos and the community do have a voice" (Santiago 2016). In addition to increasing voter turnout in order to elect Paul Penzone in place of Arpaio, Arizona's Latino population and the coalition of Latino-driven advocacy groups also greatly pushed back on Arpaio and his illegal immigration enforcement tactics. Groups such as Puente formed in 2007 in response to Arpaio's embrace and use of 287(g), a federal program that enabled Maricopa County deputies to act as de facto immigration agents (Kauffman 2016). Latino-driven organizations pushed Latino-centered politics and "successfully engaged 10 different unions, including the American Federation of Government Employees (AFGE), a union that represents Border Patrol, to be part of this campaign to mobilize Latino voters and kick out Arpaio" (Ballesteros 2017).

Arpaio's lack of support was further compounded by the burden his legal issues imposed on the people of Maricopa County. Two weeks before election day, Arpaio was charged with contempt of court for ignoring an injunction to halt traffic stops of motorists suspected of being in the country illegally in 2016. He had been under federal investigation for racial profiling since 2009, and his office was also accused of mismanaging its finances, ignoring sex crime investigations, and making politically motivated arrests (Wyloge 2012).

Historically, Arpaio had been under criminal investigation without consequence of charges or losing his seat in office, but that changed when he refused to stop carrying out patrols that targeted Latinos. This final charge before the 2016 election further motivated voters to end his term and corruption of Maricopa County. Additionally, his lawsuit for targeting Latinos had cost taxpayers more than $41 million. All in all, his legal fees including other expenses totaled $80 million in taxpayer dollars (Jordan 2016). Arpaio's defeat in the 2016 race signifies an important turn for the people of Maricopa County. For many years, Arpaio racially targeted Latinos and wreaked havoc in the community. Maricopa County's stance in 2016 to vote for Paul Penzone and end Arpaio's corrupt seven terms as sheriff stands as a major victory for Latinos in Maricopa County.

On August 27, 2017, despite losing public support and being found guilty of numerous violations, Joe Arpaio was pardoned by President Trump. Via Twitter, Trump stated, "Throughout his time as sheriff, Arpaio continued his life's work of protecting the public from the scourges of crime and illegal immigration." Further, the statement read, "Sheriff Joe Arpaio is now 85 years old, and after more than 50 years of admirable service to our nation, he is (a) worthy candidate for a Presidential pardon." Joe Arpaio responded via Twitter: "Thank you @realdonaldtrump for seeing my conviction for what it is: a political witch hunt by holdovers in the Obama justice department" (Kelsey 2017).

In 2016, advocacy groups in Arizona were pivotal in ousting Sheriff Arpaio from office, and they also helped lead the fight for a living wage in the passing of a key piece of legislation that aimed to reduce poverty and greatly impacted a large part of the NAM: Proposition 206. The "Fight for $15" campaign, a national movement advocating for a $15 minimum wage and the right to unionize, was originally initiated by two hundred fast-food employees in New York City in 2012, but quickly expanded to more than 230 cities across the United States (Stuart 2019). In 2016, Arizona's minimum wage was $8.05, which totaled around $16,744 per year for a full-time employee—a figure very close to the national poverty line as defined by the U.S. government.

In Arizona, a variety of professionals such as fast-food workers, grocery clerks, childcare workers, home healthcare specialists, and college instructors came together in their movement to raise the state's minimum wage. These different groups of low-income earners with seemingly not a lot in common were united by the fact that they were victims of a steady decline in real wages. Through the backing, leadership, and persistent organizing by grassroots organizations such as Living United for Change in Arizona (LUCHA), voters in the State of Arizona approved Proposition 206 and initiated the yearly incremental increase of Arizona's minimum wage and the mandate of paid sick time for workers: "That proposition boosted the state's minimum to $10 in 2017 from $8.05 an hour in 2016, followed by an increase to $10.50 in 2018 and $11 in 2019. The fourth hike will take the minimum wage to $12 an hour in 2020" (Gundran 2018).

The passing of Proposition 206 in Arizona was motivated by a desire for fairness and to reverse decades of wage declines that had caused full-time employees—considered "low-income earners"—to face great financial hardship. Full-time employees receiving low wages could not realistically pay for basic needs like shelter and food. At the wages set before the passing of Proposition 206, an average single adult living in Maricopa County would have to find housing for approximately $654 a month—a daunting task in today's economy. According to research conducted by the Living Wage Project, an initiative of the Massachusetts Institute of Technology, workers in the lower quarter of the earnings distribution would have to make "about $9.20 an hour to pay for food, medical care, housing, transportation, and other basic needs. . . . To add one child, workers need to earn $19.87. For 2 children: $25.43" (Stuart 2019).

Latest Phase of Latino Politics: 2018 Rising American Electorate

The Rising American Electorate (RAE) is a segment of the voting population that consists of young people of all races, communities of color, and unmarried women of all races. This portion of the population has been slowly increasing in size for over a decade. In 2016, it became a majority of the electorate for the first time in history. In 2004, the RAE made up 45 percent of the voting eligible population, and in just fourteen years grew to 62 percent in 2018. The non-RAE population, on the other hand, held 55 percent of the eligible population in 2004 and in 2018 reduced to only 38 percent (Voter Participation Project 2019). The sheer size and quick growth of this sector positions it as important to influencing both midterm and general elections if voters turn out and if groups make it a priority to campaign to them.

During the 2018 midterms, the RAE held almost 142 million eligible voters at 62 percent of the voting eligible population. Although they held such a large proportion of the voting power, they were only 53 percent of the actual total electorate: their largest share of any midterm election to date. Further, only 46 percent of these voters turned out to vote, compared to the 66 percent of non-RAE voters who turned out (Voter Participation Project 2019). Yet, even with this discrepancy (low proportion of possible voter to who actually voted), the RAE was highly influential in the elections. The perceived change that this populace could set in motion if its voting power is utilized is very important to the future of American politics.

The immense potential power of this population has been recognized by both the Republican and Democratic parties. The past decade has seen a shift by grassroots civic engagement groups toward focusing on voter registration and voter education among the RAE. In recent elections, this has led to an increase in voter turnout, but there continues to be a large discrepancy in the number of eligible voters and the actual number of RAEs who register to vote and those who actually turn out to the polls. Important to note is that non-RAEs register and vote at higher proportions than their RAE counterparts, diminishing the overall power that the RAEs derive from their population size. There are multiple reasons for their lack of registration and low voting rate, but the main issues are that they tend to be of lower socioeconomic status compared to non-RAE members, meaning that they are less educated overall, have less access to information about voting, and less access to resources. They also change residence more often than non-RAE members, making it difficult to register and stay registered to vote (Voter Participation Project 2019).

Interestingly, research has shown that the RAE population faces three main hurdles to fully utilizing their voting power in the elections: being underregistered, underinformed, and under attack. Much of the RAE population remains unregistered to vote, with Latinos, mostly among young people, whose lack of registration gives non-RAE members an advantage at the polls. Secondly, members of the RAE do not receive the necessary information regarding how to vote. Research by the Voter Participation Center (VPC), an online civic engagement organization, found that the number-one reason RAE members did not vote was because they did not know enough about the election, the candidates, or about the policy debates on the issues that they do care about (Voter Participation Project 2019). Not knowing the procedures or what documents they need to vote and/or how to vote in elections discourages people from voting because they do not feel included in the process or confident enough to register or go to a poll. The lack of knowledge about the dynamic voting procedures, the registration process, and the procedure once they arrive at the polls leads to the next point: the RAE population is under attack.

In many states, it is becoming more and more difficult to vote, due to various and more stringent voter ID laws, shifting precinct boundaries, frequently changing rules about voter registration, legalized voter intimidation, cutbacks in early voting and vote-by-mail, lack of voting sites, inequitable distribution of voting machines, and long lines on election day due to inequitable resources, to name a few (Voter Participation Project 2019). These imposed obstacles are calculated and planned attacks on the RAE population. If the RAE is consistently challenged in this way, then it is less likely that they will seek out resources to learn how to register and get their votes included, leading to a suppression of their voices. Of importance is that the states that tend to pass new restrictions on voting and make it harder for the RAE to vote are states that have the greatest growth and turnout among African Americans and Latinos, Arizona being one of these (2019).

To combat the major barriers faced by the RAE, national grassroots civic engagement organizations are focused on this population as a whole. According to Page Gardner, founder and president of VPC, "Systemic, structural barriers can still limit the RAE's participation in elections. That's why we can't be complacent. We must register more voters–especially those from traditionally underrepresented groups–and provide them with the information they need to cast their ballots in 2020" (Voter Participation Project 2019). Working to encourage the RAE to register to vote and then to vote is vital for multiple reasons, but, most important, because in 2020 they will be a majority share of the electorate, with a projected 64 percent of the population eligible to vote in 2020 and a predicted 56 percent turning out. It is imperative that the nation's elected officials reflect the general population in both midterm and general elections. The work done by these grassroots civic engagement organizations made a vast difference in the 2018 midterm election across the nation, as well as locally for Arizona. Their "get-out-the-vote" activities for the Rising American Electorate increased their voter electorate to 53 percent, with 46 percent casting votes (2019). In Arizona, this meant that Latinos dramatically increased the number of actual voters, leading to changes to the Arizona political landscape in the 2018 midterm elections.

Arizona Democrats: A Surging Turnout and Electoral Gains in 2018

In Arizona, the RAE—and, more specifically, the Latino population—saw large increases in voter turnout. During the midterms, the long-predicted "sleeping giant" Latino voting bloc began to show signs of awakening and flexing its muscles in local and statewide-level elections. Due to this emergence, the 2018 elections were seen as successful for the Arizona Democratic Party and served as evidence for many of the bullish voices that predicted and pushed the narrative that Arizona would evolve from a "tough-minded conservative" state to a state that is in transition and ready to "flip." A multitude of factors played a part in Arizona's electoral "blue wave," including the work of national, state-wide, and local grassroots civic engagement organizations to increase voter registration and voter turnout among Latinos and the RAE. Additionally, the state's rapidly changing demographics; Donald Trump's continued vilification of and antipathy toward immigrants and minorities; the lessening of obstacles and improvements in accessibility and opportunities for eligible voters to cast their vote through utilizing the vote-by-mail option and enrolling in the Permanent Early Voting List (PEVL); the newly elected Maricopa county recorder's ability to use emergency voting centers if and when needed on election day (as of 2016); and the continued outreach, organization, and mobilization of the Latino vote by national and local grassroots voter registration groups such as Mijente, Mi Familia Vota, PAZ, LUCHA, Puente, Latino Vote Project, and One Arizona and their coalition of Latino voter-registration groups played a major role in the rise in voters and the success of the Democratic Party.

In Arizona's rapidly changing demographic landscape, Latinos now make up about one in three of the state's populace and are growing at a faster rate than any other segment of the population (Santos et al. 2019). Further, Arizona is predicted to be a majority-minority state by 2030 (2019). Due to an already expansive and rapidly growing populace, the Latino voting bloc played an integral part in the Democratic party's statewide and local level victories during the 2018 midterms. Further, Latinos are the youngest and fastest-growing segment of Arizona's population, and their improved political organization and participation by grassroots civic engagement organizations led to an increase in voter turnout by 22 percent from 2014 to 2018, with 75 percent of their vote going to Democratic candidates. Importantly, the vote of young Latinos played a pivotal role in the statewide elections of senator Kyrsten Sinema (D) and Arizona's secretary of state Katie Hobbs (D).

In this key federal-level Senate race, Sinema, an activist-turned-moderate "Blue Dog" centrist and an openly bisexual woman, was able to claim the seat vacated by Republican Jeff Flake to become the first woman ever elected to the Senate from Arizona. In another pivotal statewide race for Arizona Democrats, Katie Hobbs defeated Republican Steve Gaynor by less than 1 percent to secure the Arizona secretary of state office for the Democrats for the first time since 1995. Both Sinema and Hobbs were victorious due in large part to their ability to outperform their Republican counterparts with independent voters, persuading some moderate Republicans to cross party lines by embracing political moderation, emphasizing bipartisanship, and largely avoiding ideological issues (Allen 2018).

According to the digital encyclopedia of American politics and elections Ballotpedia, Democrats gained four seats in the state House of Representatives during the 2018 election and are now only two seats away from being the majority for the first time in over 50 years, since 1966: "The Republican majority in the House of Representatives was reduced from 35–25 to 31–29" ("Arizona House of Representatives" n.d.). Democrats successfully defeated three Republican incumbents during the general election and only one Democratic incumbent was defeated during the primary. One of the newly elected Democratic members of the Arizona House of Representatives representing District 30 was Raquel Terán, the former Arizona director of the civic engagement organization Mi Familia Vota. Terán, originally from Douglas, Arizona, was previously a community organizer and civil rights activist who strongly opposed SB 1070, which she deemed to have an "anti-immigrant sentiment" (Santos et al. 2019). Along with fellow Democrat Robert Meza, Terán defeated Republican Gary Spears in the 2018 general election. She was elected to replace state representative Tony Navarrete (D), who instead successfully ran for state senate ("Arizona House of Representatives" 2018). Terán's election-day victory served as further evidence of Arizona's changing political landscape. Furthermore, Arizona Democrats did not lose any of their state senate seats in the 2018 midterms: "The Republican majority in the State Senate did not change, remaining at 17 Republicans to 13 Democrats" ("Arizona House of Representatives" n.d.).

Many members of this new wave of Latino politicians in Arizona initially entered politics to oppose the Brewer and Arpaio era, which was characterized by tough jail policies, a strong anti-immigrant posture, and the passing of draconian immigration bill SB 1070. According to Fernanda Santos et al. (2019), these Latinos utilized "the lessons they learned in organizing against the immigration crackdown to catapult themselves into elected state and local office." At the local level, Latinos such as migrant rights activist Carlos García, the former longtime director of Puente, and Betty Guardado, a hotel housekeeper-turned-union organizer with Unite Here Local 11, a union representing airport, hotel, and food service workers, were voted into the Phoenix City Council during the 2018 midterms as the District 8 and District 5 representatives. Both were among the increasing number of Latino community organizers and activists to become elected officials. They ran and were elected with the intention of not only entering the halls of power, but, according to Santos et al. (2019), of utilizing their newfound positions to not only apply pressure from the outside but also "infiltrate these systems and do something radically different" to ultimately, "dismantle this system that was created to hurt our people and to get rid of us."

Other Latino civil rights activists were elected into office during the 2018 midterm election, including Regina Romero, from Somerton, Arizona, the cofounder of the Arizona Association of Latino Elected Officials (AALEO) and previous Latino outreach director for the Center for Biological Diversity, who was the first Latina elected to the Tucson City Council and, in the 2018 midterms, was elected to be Tucson's first Latina mayor. When Romero opted to run for mayor, she selected Lane Santa Cruz to replace her on the

Tucson City Council. According to Santos et al. (2019), the groundbreaking Romero touted Santa Cruz's cultural, educational, and activist background as examples of some of the many reasons that she believed Santa Cruz to be the ideal replacement for her. Santa Cruz "grew up in one of the poorest and most heavily Hispanic corners of Tucson and, armed with a Ph.D. in education, worked for more than 10 years as an advocate for her neighbors, many of them undocumented as her parents once were" (2019).

Ultimately, the Latino vote played a pivotal role in all facets of the 2018 midterm elections in Arizona. From state senate to local council, facilitating major changes for the Latino community. Additionally, although Arizona continually has more registered Republicans than Democrats by a wide margin (roughly 136,000 more registered Republican voters in Arizona), these Democratic gains in the Arizona House of Representatives, U.S. Senate, and at the local level during the midterms allowed Arizona to be labeled by political pundits as a state in transition heading toward becoming a purple, battleground state (Allen 2018).

In response to the electoral gains made by the Arizona Democrats during the 2018 midterm elections, Arizona's Republican party proposed public policies that would essentially place new restrictions on voting and therefore make political participation more difficult. As discussed earlier, these restrictions, also known as voter suppression tactics, have been implemented throughout multiple states across the United States to discourage the minority vote and the Rising American Electorate.

Research carried out by the VPC has concluded that states looking to suppress votes do so by utilizing the following tactics: "Ever-more-stringent voter ID laws, constantly-changing rules about voter registration requirements, shifting precinct boundaries, cutbacks in early voting and vote-by-mail, legalized voter intimidation, inequitable distribution of voting machines leading to long lines on Election Day" (Voter Participation Project 2019). One of the study's most troubling conclusions regarding the states passing new voter suppression laws is that they "tend to be the ones with the greatest turnout and growth among African-Americans and Latinos" (2019).

Arizona, like California, Colorado, Nevada, and New Mexico, has a thriving Latino population and made large gains in moving their state's political landscape "from red to purple and then, eventually, blue" (Shogren 2016).

State data from the 2018 midterm elections revealed that, overall, Arizona Democrats organized and galvanized their constituents into registering to vote at higher rates than their Republican counterparts: seventy thousand (7 percent) to fifty thousand (5 percent) in Maricopa County alone. Latinos in the State of Arizona will make up approximately one-third of all Arizonans by 2030 (Griffin et al. 2019). According to Elizabeth Shogren (2016), Arizona's election laws "make it harder for Latinos to be elected to local and state office: Because Arizona voters elect two representatives to the state Legislature from relatively large districts, minorities are at a disadvantage."

Furthermore, Republicans have proposed new voting rights laws that complicate voters' ability to cast an early ballot in order to remove registered voters from the PEVL—specifically, voters who signed up to cast mail ballots but did not use this method of voting. State senator Michelle Ugenti-Rita proposed Senate Bill 1046 (SB 1046) in order to purge voters from the PEVL if they do not cast an early ballot for two consecutive election cycles. While many believed that the proposed legislation by Arizona Republicans would curb voting rights and discourage younger, nonwhite, and lower-income voters from voting—those less likely to vote for Republicans—the state's Republican legislators maintained that their proposed laws were put forth in order to preserve the integrity of voter rolls and to prevent in-person voter fraud.

Additionally, Arizona Republicans put forward several additional bills that were heavily criticized by voting rights groups. The eventually rejected legislation would impose obstacles on voters that would ultimately lead to voter suppression. For example, public officials wanted to ban the ability of workers to get paid for any voter registration forms that they submit (López et al. 2019), place a limit on the county recorder's use of emergency voting centers, and set parameters on the timeline for "curing" mail-in-ballots that flagged and/or questioned the signature of the voter (Gardiner 2018). Lastly, the lone bill proposed by Senator Ugenti-Rita that was approved by the legislative body called for Arizona "voters to produce ID to cast ballots at in-person early voting sites" (Giles 2019). Many of Senator Ugenti-Rita's counterparts criticized her proposal of Senate Bill 1072 (SB 1072) as a way of excluding elderly and lower-income voters that did not have the means to access a driver's license as a form of identification.

Future Implications

The 2018 midterm elections in Arizona saw a significant shift in votes coming from the RAE and the Latino population in particular. Efforts by civic engagement organizations aimed at Latinos and the RAE proved successful in their mission to register and educate voters and oppose voter suppression policies. Moving forward, it is important that organizations targeting the Latino vote in Arizona include the other members of the RAE. It is through this shift in focus that the RAE will be able to elect appointed officials that reflect the diverse communities that make up the United States.

In Arizona, the political reactions to these anti-immigrant proposals continue to be intriguing, from a theoretical, historical, and applied perspective. Overall, the anti-immigrant agenda has actually mobilized individuals into a formidable political force, galvanizing a backlash by nontraditional political players such as noncitizens, students, immigrant women, small church congregations, grassroots organizations, and young people of color.

These nontraditional activists are protesting and demonstrating in numbers never before witnessed in the State of Arizona. Furthermore, traditional political players such as elected officials have called for economic boycotts, protests, and campaigns to counter these proposals. Numerous surveys illustrate that registered Latino voters frustrated with the anti-immigrant rhetoric voted to oppose these measures and considered immigration an important policy agenda. A number of established lobby groups and organizations also got involved in the political process, pushing to stop these proposals. The changes in demographics and citizenship status, as well as the ever-evolving forces and events that galvanize Latinos, means that Latino politics can and should be analyzed from a variety of perspectives.

It appears that the boycotts were successful. For instance, in 2014, the legislature introduced a bill that would allow businesses to deny service if they felt the customer violated their moral or religious conscience. After SB 1062 passed through the Senate and was sent to the governor to sign, national and international attention focused once again on Arizona. This time, however, the Arizona Chamber of Commerce was quick to point out that bad publicity—looking like a state that was intolerant—was bad for business. The governor ultimately did not sign the bill.

During recent elections, DREAMers—young individuals hoping to get legalized status because they were brought to the United States through no fault of their own—campaigned and asked constituents to only support elected officials who backed comprehensive immigration reform. A new generation of young Latino activists, politicians, and entrepreneurs emerged as well, and organizations established to protect the rights of immigrants have also grown in numbers. Coalitions of churches and ecumenical efforts have come together to protect immigrants' rights and to provide different forms of assistance to immigrants.

Latinos are rapidly increasing their demographic presence in the United States and will be an important group in determining the future of the United States. The reason they are so important is because of the political power that they represent through votes. As they increase in number, Latinos will wield greater power, and politicians in office as well as aspiring politicians will need to take a look at the needs of Latinos in order to secure their own political power. Latinos have been galvanized by the anti-immigrant movement; simply put, for some, anti-immigration comes across as anti-Latino. In Arizona, the transformation of Latino politics that really began growing exponentially in the early to mid-2000s continues in the current political climate.

In the 2020 presidential election, Joe Biden turned the State of Arizona blue for the first time since 1996. According to AP VoteCast, the partisan shift was largely attributed to Latinos (Vinopal 2020). Latinos make up about 23 percent of the state population and 33 percent of Maricopa County. 60 percent of all residents in Arizona live in Maricopa County, which had the largest proportion of votes overall. The AP survey found that 66 percent of the Latino population voted for Biden while 33 percent voted for Trump. The survey also found that the support for Biden from Latinos was significantly important in the 2020 election. Overall, white Arizona voters was much closer. That is, 47 percent of white voters supported Trump, while 51 percent supported Biden. Those surveyed also thought that Trump's rhetoric and emphasis on immigration was no longer as important. Generally, all respondents thought that the federal government should be more focused on COVID-19 even if it hurts the economy (2020).

CHAPTER 5

Interview with Randy Pérez

We end our book with an interview with Randy Pérez, democracy director with LUCHA and ACE. He sheds light on some of the political organizing strategies in Arizona. We think Randy best represents the future of Latino politics in Arizona.

Zoom meeting transcription: Lisa Magaña, César S. Silva, and Randy Pérez

MAGAÑA: What are your duties with LUCHA?

PÉREZ: I handle all of the voting rights work. That includes the state legislature, it includes county recorders, elections administration policy, the secretary of state. I'm also a registered lobbyist for LUCHA. So, I spend a lot of time working on minute policy issues, trying to make sure that the democracy organizing and the democracy space that we work in is inclusive and accessible as possible. A lot of times the democracy work, or the theme of democracy, is owned by think tanks or universities, but not by folks that are impacted. So, like all the work that we do at LUCHA, we want folks that are most impacted by attacks on our right to vote to be the ones that are centered in the work that we're doing.

MAGAÑA: The book that we are working on is that there's been various phases of Latino politics. Most recently, I would say in the mid-1990s, when immigration became this national issue, it sort of galvanized all of us, not just people of Mexican origin, and, of course, non-Latino as well.

SILVA: The New American voters, is that what you're saying?

MAGAÑA: Yeah. Would you agree with that? What are your thoughts about this "new American electorate," correct?

PÉREZ: Yeah, "New American Majority." So, I think it's a really interesting framing and is super helpful because, you know, it's been ten years since 1070 this year. So, there's been a lot of anniversary work that's been going on. A lot of recentering of 1070 and the conversation of where we are. But, also, I think folks like me that are younger and newer are trying to push "What do the next ten years look like?," right? So, always being routed in that 1070 was the galvanizing moment that helped create LUCHA, Puente. Puente, I think, was there starting in 2006, perhaps. But, you know, where do we go from here. So, grounding all the work that we do at the legislature, and it's been ten years since this moment. This is what we created. This is the conditions that we've created. Here's where we still need to go to meet the values of that. Um, but, so, I've been spending a lot of time thinking about 1070 and thinking about what it means for someone like me who was in Wisconsin when this happened, right. I was in Wisconsin. I was fourteen when 1070 happened. I knew what Arpaio was, I knew what 1070 was from the news. Um, but I still feel it, right? I still feel the aftershocks of 1070, I was thrown out of the state legislature for testifying on a bill . . . during a fight where we were actually able to kill what we called SB 1070 2.0, which is essentially a city referral . . . so it reared . . . it's actually a beautiful moment we had this year, right. SB 1070 reared its ugly head in the form of a sanctuary city referral that Governor Ducey in this state of the state address said he was going to put on the ballot. We looked at this policy, we analyzed it with all the new capacity that they never had in 2010, right. We said, "What does this actually mean?" Saw that this would essentially enshrine 1070 in the constitution as an amendment if passed by the voters. Saw that there was an election year ploy from the governor to gin up his base in order to help elect Trump, to help elect McSally, to elect Republicans up and down the ticket because they are worried. And we said, "Not again." So, not only did we bring in all the same partners from 2010 in the fight—faith leaders, community organizations—but we also brought in business leaders that we have relationships with now. Not just the Hispanic chamber but the Arizona Chamber of Commerce. We had polling that we were able to do that showed this was unpopular with voters . . . and we killed that within five weeks of some of the most intense political organizing that I have ever seen and been a part of.

MAGAÑA: Ok, so, sanctuary city, that's interesting. You're thinking of it as a new SB 1070, I like that.

PÉREZ: I think that for a long time . . . to show that you were a part of the movement, you had to really be about it, right? And you had to be from it. I'm here home right now in Wisconsin. I'm in rural Wisconsin. I'm the only Pérez in my family. I had no conceptualization of what it meant to be Latino until I moved to Arizona and took your class even, starting learning from folks that were organizing. I still had no conceptualization of what it meant to be in a space of folks who are directly impacted until I really started working at LUCHA. You know the folks that are coming in and out every single day that are documented, undocumented, mixed status, that have been criminalized for their very existence. For me to be allowed to enter into that space is new . . . I'm one of the . . . and I still struggle with that. Some folks still struggle with me being a part of that, right. I'm sure there are some folks who will struggle with me being in your book about the history of Latino politics in Arizona.

MAGAÑA: . . . well, we'll kick their a**.

PÉREZ: And the reason I say that is because the definition of what it meant to be Latino has changed, right? And there are starting to be more folks like me who it is a part of our identity . . . and are mixed than there are folks that are 100 percent, goes back multiple generations . . . to any Latino country . . . Spanish speaking was a qualification for this type of work. I don't speak a lick of Spanish. I understand it but I can't speak it . . . so it's a shift that's happening, and I've tried to help bring more folks in because we were excluded in some ways too. And I totally get that, because these spaces have to be protected and real and rooted in family and culture. But now we have to grow.

MAGAÑA: So why do you think it's changed? The reality of demographic shifts and . . .

PÉREZ: I think it's had to change because the demographics is just one, there are going to be more folks who have heritage like mine . . . that are rooted in their Latino identity, especially in their organizing and politics and racial analysis that we have. Then there are folks who aren't 100 percent certain of anything anymore, or who can claim that. I also think that capacity will be an issue forever in your organizing. If you're intentionally excluding folks that are with you on things because they don't have the exact same upbringing as you. Now, do I think that those folks who are most impacted should be the ones that we have to continue to build relationships with, listen to, and learn from. I learn so much listening to folk's stories, and it's my job to elevate those stories. My story is less, coming from privilege, is less relevant to the work that we do. It's important and I've come to see that it's important because I'm a contributor to that work, but I would much rather center the folks that are really, really struggling and that's what we're trying to give voice to. But you have to trust me with your story first.

MAGAÑA: Ok, so . . . now . . . you're certainly . . . you're focusing more on electoral politics and voting, right? That's your focus right now with this campaign.

PÉREZ: I definitely do work that is related to increasing access to voting. Whether it's killing voter suppression bills at the capital, pushing for proactive democracy of forums, working with the secretary of state and county recorders on election policies that bring more folks in . . . but we are also trying to think about how do we get folks that cannot vote to participate, right? That's a really big thing that we are working on. We are thinking about undocumented and municipal voting . . . we are thinking about . . . felon reenfranchisement and even if you don't have your right to vote, we . . . it's our responsibility and duty at LUCHA to create a space for you where you can actively participate in our democracy . . . I play with the word "democracy" a lot because I feel as if it's not been inclusive at all for folks. I was doing a presentation for indigenous youth from Salt River back in September and

I have this presentation about the history of voting rights in Arizona and I have a question that I always ask, and it's "What does democracy mean to you?" Their question back to me with almost in unison in almost seventy young people is "What is democracy?" This was a completely foreign concept to them.

MAGAÑA: So, what do you say?

PÉREZ: So, I told them, I said, you know at first I was stumped . . . I was just shocked, and that was my blind spot. Like, I'm using this word and assuming folks are with me. And I said to them, "It is whatever you can make of it." Right? "It's yours." We talked a lot about how they are already participating in their democracy by being present, by learning, it was like a capital day. So, these were the best youth that they were able to put together . . . but they didn't have that ownership, right? So, we even played with the thesis of "own your democracy," right? There are folks who do not want you to own it, they don't want you to participate. If we can provide avenues for you to own it and feel it and live it, it becomes like second nature to you. So, that's been a big thing we are working on too.

PÉREZ: The future of Latino politics will always be about building power for our communities, with our communities, and expanding the definition of what that community is. I think that that's going to be the key, is if we can as a community come together and say, "We need to bring new people in, we need to expand our definition of what this means, we need to accept some change, we need to continue to ask tough questions and making sure that we build trust." But that's what I think the future is. But when I think about the next ten years, and what we want to build at LUCHA, it's really, how do we continue to push the envelope with the power that we've built that allows more folks into the process.

So, ten years ago you could never dream about doing a campaign for undocumented municipal voting, right? The same way you couldn't have dreamed about doing a minimum wage increase in 2016. But we have built the tools, the power, and the know-how, and the capacity by which we can now execute our wildest dreams, because we have the resources to do so. So, I think we're going to keep dreaming really big, I think we're going to keep fighting, I think we're going to keep holding folks accountable. I also think we're going to start getting into some institutional positions of power and start to play the inside/outside game. You see that when we elected representative Raquel Terán, who is on our LUCHA board, long-time community member and activist and leader. Now she is in the state legislature, taking a totally different view than typically would be taken by members of that body. So, are we going to start electing our own people . . . ? And you see the way that Carlos Garcia being there is changing the conversation completely and the narrative completely on what aid and who should be included in what aid during this moment. There would be no movement, I would imagine, for undocumented folks to receive city aid without Carlos being in there and saying, "No way. I'm not voting on anything without including everyone from our community."

SILVA: Are you guys having a good amount of success getting undocumented so far, and what are some of the things you are doing to attempt to, or, if you haven't, what are you doing that is working for you, to get the undocumented community to come out and participate? Because one of the things I talk about in my dissertation is the idea of traditional participation, defined traditionally by political scientists. I'm trying to say the reason people think the Latino community does not participate at the levels expected from such a large community is because I think the participation definition is kind of skewed to not represent this community. The participation for undocumented isn't going to be counted. No one is going to be there and say, "Oh, these DREAMers," or the other millions of people who are not considered in the DREAMer's title who do participate . . . or people who do participate because they have mixed status family members and what not. So, what I'm trying to do is get a truer representation of Latino participation. What are some of the things you guys have done to get DREAMers or undocumented in general to participate?

PÉREZ: Yes, I think that's a really beautiful expansion of the definition of participation . . . I think on the voter's side, real quick, we know that turnout has gone through the roof in the Latino communities since 2010. We have the data to show that in Arizona, as a percentage of the electorate, Latinos were 27 percent of that electorate. That is a massive, massive increase from

2010, when were about 8–10 percent, perhaps. And that includes the fact that the electorate itself has grown and the participation has still gone up, which is even more wild to think about . . . yet we still have a lot of Democratic campaigns and, like, consultants that use turnout models or voter models that undersample our community so they don't receive the investment. For example, I received a model for a campaign that we were working on that's no longer in existence, where they sent us this voter model for the mail and digital and all the things they wanted to do and had the ratio break down, and I was like, "15 percent for Latinos, that's not right." So, I immediately asked Alex and said, "This can't be right." She said, "No, our data shows 27%, national data shows 21%." Yet, I was presented a model by consultants from D.C. that says it was 15%. So, what happens then? We have to rely on persuading older white people or older white independents instead of our folks, because they're not even included in the model. If you're not in the model, you're not going to get an investment, any money, any organizing . . . so, that is the disaster of the Democratic party, is that these are the models and professionals they are using and not including our people, yet they wonder why we don't show to vote and participate.

On the documented and undocumented piece, I think of . . . we have some amazing folks that are undocumented at LUCHA as members, volunteers, parents of people, and, so, I'm thinking about Maribel, right? This woman, her name is Maribel. She's amazing, I don't know how old she is, maybe late forties, early fifties, undocumented, doesn't speak English . . . she shows up every day. Every day she shows up. She will phone bank, she will canvas, she'll have one-on-ones with people, she'll bring food, she'll clean the office, she shows up for all her English classes. She's also on our endorsement committee. This is the first year that LUCHA is doing a really expensive endorsement process. We want to exert our political power to set the stage and tone for what it means to be not just Democratic but LUCHA blue is how we're putting it, and really live our values. Maribel is on the committee. She sat in a committee with me and twenty other people and in Spanish asked senior advisors from the Bernie Sanders campaign, Elizabeth Warren campaign, and Julian Castro, tough, tough questions about the minimum wage, about worker conditions, and that is more participation and more love and resilience and rigor than you will see from anybody else. I am constantly inspired by Maribel. She is amazing . . .

. . . Who is going to count [Ellie Pérez] if we don't count our own people? That is why your work is so important, why this book is so important. Because there are going to be so many folks in this book that no one has any idea the impact they are making day by day, because traditional media, white-led media, is never going to tell this story the right way. I know you know that, but I think that's why it's so important.

. . . I think that expanding the definition of participation is what I'm trying to do in our democracy program by also expanding the definition of "democracy," increasing ownership of democracy, that's why I'm grounded in the work that I do, and why I'm lucky to do it. That's why I try to use my privilege to create avenues for someone like Maribel to thrive. She's an amazing member of our committee, she's going to ask questions of candidates from across the state and hold them accountable. I know that, our people know that, and now you know that. It's traditional storytelling.

APPENDIX A

One Arizona Fact Sheet

Background

One Arizona was formed in 2010 as a direct response to the growing disenfranchisement of voters and to the attack on our Latino community in the form of SB 1070. For five years, One Arizona has worked under a successful collaborative format on civic engagement efforts in statewide, off-year and odd-year (municipal) election seasons. One Arizona's table members represent a broad tapestry of 501(c)(3)s focused on voter registration, voter engagement, voter mobilization, election protection, and issue advocacy.

One Arizona has enhanced collaboration, minimized duplication of efforts, developed best practices for data management and voter engagement, coordinated volunteer management, joint field efforts, improved evaluation measures, built rigorous accountability systems, and utilized economies of scale to reduce costs.

Since 2010, One Arizona has grown into one of the most effective c(3) civic engagement tables in the nation, as we have increased Latino political power in our state. One Arizona has run successful voter registration, permanent early voting sign-up, GOTV, voter education, and election protection work in 2010 (Midterm), 2011 (Cities of Phoenix and Tucson), 2012 (Presidential), 2013 (City of Phoenix), 2014 (Midterm), and 2015 (Cities of Phoenix and Tucson).

Accomplishments

Our efforts and strategies are focused on ensuring we build a strong grass-roots program that meets voters where they are. Here are some of our collective accomplishments:

- Knocked on nearly 700,000 doors
- Made over 800,000 phone calls
- Signed up over 110,000 Latinos to the PEVL
- Increased the number of Latinos on the PEVL from 91,000 in January 2010 to over 340,000 as of October 2015
- Registered and updated over 40,000 voter registrations
- Maintained a steady growth in the Latino electorate since 2010 (Latino vote share: 2008, 16 percent; 2010, 12 percent; 2012, 18 percent; 2014, 12 percent)
- Most important, fostered and convened a unified, coordinated front of allies and organizations focused on improving civic engagement efforts in Arizona.

Recent Developments

Since its inception, our work has centered on Latinos in Arizona. In 2014, we expanded our targeting to include a "Latino+" model, adding additional unmarried women and voters between the ages of eighteen and thirty into the universe. Additionally, we have incorporated a communications hub that works to build communications capacity in our member organizations, as well as a data and research cohort, which will likewise expose the leaders in our network to a deeper understanding of the voter file, targeting, field campaign mechanics, and even scientific experiments. The One AZ Student Vote Coalition launched in 2015 to coordinate civic engagement efforts with high school, community college, and university students and campuses. New work around service-based provider outreach expands our reach to additional low-income, working families in Arizona. Finally, a new poll monitoring effort ensuring fair access to the ballot box was implemented in 2014 as well as a voter guide focused on those issues important to our community (One Arizona 2016).

APPENDIX B

List of Organizations

Organization	Membership	Year established	Mission/goal	Website
All Voting Is Local	Arizona Georgia Nevada Pennsylvania Florida Michigan Ohio Wisconsin	2018	We fight to remove discriminatory barriers to the ballot to achieve a democracy that works for us all.	https://allvotingislocal.org/
Arizona Advocacy Network	Arizona	2002	AZAN is devoted to defending and deepening Arizona's commitment to democracy. We believe the cornerstones of a vibrant democracy are meaningful voting rights and access to the ballot, political decisions driven by voters instead of money, and a fair and independent judiciary.	https://www.azadvocacy.org/
Arizona Center for Empowerment	Arizona		ACE is a member-led social justice organization that develops and mobilizes undocumented working youth and adults, students, and LGBTQ individuals to strategically take ownership and responsibility to advance economic, social, and racial justice.	https://www.empoweraz.org/

Organization	Location	Year	Description	URL
Arizona Coalition for Change	Arizona		Empowers everyday people to transform their community through building civic power, just and equitable schools, and safer neighborhoods. We are committed to advocating for lasting progressive public policies that change the dynamics for our communities. By putting people first, we are working to develop and lift up voices of communities to take on our nation's most pressing issues.	https://www.azc4c.org/
Arizona Dream Act Coalition	Arizona immigrant youth-led organization	2009	ADAC advocates for the rights of our undocumented immigrant communities socially and politically by organizing and mobilizing our constituency through the development and fostering of Arizona leaders, promoting civic engagement and the attainment and equal access of higher education for immigrant youth, strengthening relationships with diverse intersectional communities, and providing services that advance the integration of our families.	http://www.theadac.org/
Arizona Student Association	Arizona	1974	A student-led, nonpartisan organization created to represent the collective interest of the 140,000+ university students and 400,000+ community college students in Arizona. We advocate at the local, state, and national levels for affordable and accessible higher education.	https://www.azstudents.org/

(continued)

Organization	Membership	Year established	Mission/goal	Website
Asian Pacific Community in Action	Arizona	2002	Our mission is to provide services, advocacy, and education for diverse communities, resulting in a healthier and more empowered population seeking good health. Our vision is to inspire diverse communities to seek healthier futures, to meet the health-related needs of Asian American, Native Hawaiian, and Pacific Islander (AA and NHPI) individuals and families residing in Arizona.	http://wwwapcaaz.org/
CAIR Arizona	National Organization in 20 states including Arizona	1994	CAIR's vision is to be a leading advocate for justice and mutual understanding. CAIR's mission is to enhance understanding of Islam, protect civil rights, promote justice, and empower American Muslims. La misión de CAIR es proteger las libertades civiles, mejorar la comprensión del Islam, promover la justicia, y empoderar a los musulmanes en los Estados Unidos.	https://cair-az.org/

Central Arizonans for a Sustainable Economy (CASE)	Arizona		CASE is a movement of young people and working families committed to achieving economic, social and immigrants' justice in Arizona. We are a grassroots organization led by our volunteer leaders, the majority of whom are young people trying to build a future in a state that currently provides them too few educational and economic opportunities.	http://case-az.org/
Chispa Arizona	Arizona		Chispa Arizona envisions an inclusive and reflective democracy that prioritizes communities' rights to clean air and water, healthy neighborhoods, and a safe climate for generations to come.	https://chispaaz.org/
Inter-Tribal Council of Arizona	Arizona	1952	To provide its member tribes with a united voice and the means for united action on matters that affect them collectively or individually; to provide a united voice for tribal governments located in the State of Arizona to address common issues of concerns.	https://itcaonline.com/

(continued)

Organization	Membership	Year established	Mission/goal	Website
Mi Familia Vota	Arizona California Colorado Florida Nevada Texas	2000	A national civic engagement organization that unites Latino, immigrant, and allied communities to promote social and economic justice through citizenship workshops, voter registration, and voter participation. Our mission is to build Latino political power by expanding the electorate and strengthening local infrastructures through year-round voter engagement. We are also training the next generation of leaders by opening opportunities through our youth development programs and through our Mi Familia Vota work.	https://www.mifamiliavota.org/
New American Leaders	National		Leading a movement for inclusive democracy by preparing first- and second-generation Americans to use their power and potential in elected office.	https://www.newamericanleaders.org/
OCA Greater Phoenix Asian Pacific American Advocates	National Arizona Chapter		We are an organization dedicated to advancing the social, political, and economic well-being of Asian Pacific Americans, touching tens of thousands of individuals each year through its extensive network of over one hundred chapters, affiliates, and partners from around the country.	https://www.ocaphoenix.org/

Name	Scope	Year	Description	URL
Planned Parenthood Arizona	National Arizona	1934	Planned Parenthood Arizona promotes and protects every person's freedom and right to enjoy sexual health and well-being, to make reproductive choices, and to build healthy, strong families.	https://www.planned parenthood.org/planned-parenthood-arizona
Poder in Action	Arizona	2013	We build power to disrupt and dismantle systems of oppression and determine a liberated future as people of color in Arizona.	https://www.poderinaction.org/
Progress Now Arizona	Arizona		We expose the powerful for their misdeeds and promote a vision of our state that works for everyone—regardless of who you are, who you love, how much you make, or where you're from. We work year-round to promote progressive issues and public policy solutions, to correct right-wing misinformation and to hold elected officials accountable.	https://progressnowarizona.org/
PAZ (Promise Arizona)	Arizona		Aims to unite the millions of Arizonans who reject the divisive politics of immigrant-baiting, millions who believe in treating their neighbors with fairness and dignity. These like-minded individuals share a common interest in good jobs, a robust economy, quality education, and safe communities in which to raise children. We help connect individuals who share similar goals so that they may work toward a better Arizona by investing in statewide infrastructure and training a new generation of leaders.	http://www.promiseaz.org/

(continued)

Organization	Membership	Year established	Mission/goal	Website
Protecting Arizona's Family Coalition	Arizona	2001	PAFCO is an inclusive and nonpartisan alliance of health and human service agencies, faith-based communities, and advocacy networks that advocate for vulnerable populations.	https://www.pafcoalition.org/
Puente Human Rights Movement (Puente)	Arizona	2007	The Puente Human Rights Movement is a grassroots migrant justice organization based in Phoenix, Arizona. We develop, educate, and empower migrant communities to protect and defend our families and ourselves.	http://puenteaz.org/
Rural Arizona Engagement (RAZE)	Arizona		RAZE's mission is to educate, advocate, and coordinate in rural communities so they may gain access to civic education, engagement opportunities and voter registration.	https://www.raze.org/

APPENDIX C

List of Laws

- In 2000, Arizona passed Proposition 203, which stated that all public schooling, K–12, was to be instructed in English only.
- In 2004, Proposition 200 was passed, which made it mandatory for people to verify their identity in order to receive government subsidies and also charged government employees with misdemeanors if they provided services to anyone believed to be undocumented.
- In 2005, the Coyote Law was passed. This policy made "smuggling undocumented persons across the border a felony, authorized local police to enforce immigration law, and classified persons being smuggled as co-conspirators" (Szkupinski-Quiroga, Medina, and Glick 2014).
- Following this, the increased anti-immigrant sentiment that was spreading across Arizona became more profound with the enactment of Proposition 100, Proposition 102, Proposition 103, and Proposition 300 in 2006:
  - Proposition 100 denied bail for immigrants who were unlawfully in the United States on the premise that "the proof is evident or the presumption great" that the person is guilty of the offense charged.
  - Proposition 102 denied unauthorized immigrants from bringing and receiving monetary compensation from civil cases. This policy excluded immigrants from filing claims of wrongdoing against them in the workplace and beyond.

- Proposition 103, also known as the "English-only Law," made English Arizona's official state language and required all official state business, including court activities and government departments that work to protect workers' rights, to be completed in English.
- Proposition 300 made persons without legal status ineligible for in-state tuition grants, scholarships, and financial aid. This policy banned undocumented immigrants and those who were born out of the country, but who otherwise have lived in Arizona their whole life, from receiving funding to better their education.
- In 2007, Governor Napolitano signed House Bill 2779 (HB 2279), which required employers to verify that their employees are in the country legally.
- In 2008, Arizona passed the Legal Arizona Workers Act (LAWA), which required all employers to utilize the identity and immigration status verification system ("E-verify") with all new hires.
- In 2010, Senate Bill 1070 (SB 1070) was authored by state senator Russell Pearce and passed.

REFERENCES

Adande, J. A. 2010. "Suns Using Jerseys to Send Message." ESPN, May 4, 2010, www
.espn.com/nba/playoffs/2010/columns/story?columnist=adande_ja&page=sarver
-100504.

Allen, Samantha. 2018. "Kyrsten Sinema's Election Win in Arizona Is a Big, Bisexual
Leap Forward." Daily Beast, November 13, 2018. https://www.thedailybeast.com
/kyrsten-sinemas-election-win-in-arizona-is-a-big-bisexual-leap-forward.

Alonzo, Monica. 2012. "SB 1070 Fuels a Movement of New Voters." *Phoenix New Times*,
July 5, 2012. http://www.phoenixnewtimes.com/news/sb-1070-fuels-movement-of
-new-voters- 6454767.

Alto Arizona! n.d. "About SB 1070." Accessed November 16, 2020. http://www.alto
arizona.com/sb1070.html.

Aizenman, N. C. 2009. "Report Cites Problems In ICE Training Program; GAO Says
Key Controls Are Missing." *Washington Post*, March 4, 2009. https://www.city
-data.com/forum/illegal-immigration/583648-report-cites-problems-ice-training
-program.html.

American History Museum. 2010. "Bittersweet Harvest: The Bracero Program, 1942–
1964." September 9, 2009–January 3, 2010. http://www.si.edu/Exhibitions/Details
/Bittersweet-Harvest-The-Bracero-Program-1942-1964-4529.

American Immigration Council. 2013. "How DACA is Impacting the Lives of Those Who
are Now DACAmented: Preliminary Findings from the National UnDACAmented
Research Project." August 15, 2013. https://www.americanimmigrationcouncil.org
/research/how-daca-impacting-lives-those-who-are-now-dacamented.

American Immigration Council. 2020. "The 287(g) Program: An Overview." July 2, 2020. www.americanimmigrationcouncil.org/research/287g-program-immigration.

Anti-Defamation League (ADL). n.d. "Myths and Facts about Immigrants and Immigration (En Español)." Accessed November 16, 2020. https://www.adl.org/resources /fact-sheets/myths-and-facts-about-immigrants-and-immigration-en-espanol.

Anzaldúa, Gloria. 1987. *Borderlands: The New Mestiza = La frontera.* San Francisco Spinsters/Aunt Lute.

Arizona House of Representatives. n.d. Accessed November 16, 2020. https://ballot pedia.org/Arizona_House_of_Representatives.

Arizona State Legislature. 2011. "Sheriff Joseph M. Arpaio." https://www.azleg.gov /JBSAC/MemberBioTemplate.asp?id=3 (link inactive).

"Arizona Primary: Republicans Playing Immigration Policy Card Still Draws Voters." 2016. National Public Radio, March 20, 2016. http://www.npr.org/2016/03 /20/471161667/arizonaprimaryrepublicans-playing-immigration-policy-card-still -draws voters.

Avalos, Manuel, and Lisa Magaña. 2013. "Proposition 187 All Over Again." In *Immigration and the Border: Politics and Policy in the New Latino Century*, edited by David Leal. Notre Dame, Ind.: University of Notre Dame Press, https://www.amazon.com /Immigration-Border-Politics-Century-Perspectives/dp/0268013357/ref=tmm _pap_swatch_0?_encoding=UTF8&qid=&sr= (accessed November 16, 2020).

Avalos, Manuel, Lisa Magaña, and Adrian Pantoja. 2010. "The Latino Vote in Arizona." In *Beyond the Barrio: Latinos in the 2004 Election*, edited by Rodolfo de la Garza, Louis De Sipio and David Leal. Notre Dame, Ind.: University of Notre Dame Press, https://www.amazon.com/Beyond-Barrio-Latinos-Elections-Perspectives /dp/0268025991/ref=sr_1_1?dchild=1&keywords=In+Beyond+the+Barrio%3A +Latinos+in+the+2004+Election&qid=1605544622&s=books&sr=1-1 (accessed November 16, 2020).

Ayón, David, and George Pla. 2018. *Power Shift: How Latinos in California Transformed Politics in America.* Berkeley, Calif.: Institute of Governmental Studies.

AZ Big Media. 2018. "Poll Finds Latino Voters Being Ignored in Lead-Up to 2018 Elections." September 5, 2018. https://azbigmedia.com/business/politics/poll-finds -latino-voters-being-ignored-in-lead-up-to-2018-elections/.

Ballesteros, Carlos. 2017. "Attacks on Immigrants Are Attacks on Workers—A Longtime Labor and Community Organizer Responds to Trump's Anti-immigrant Measures." *In These Times*, February 22, 2017. http://inthesetimes.com/article /19880/trump-immigration-labor-sheriff-joe-arpaio-daca.

Balletopedia. n.d. "Arizona State Senate." https://ballotpedia.org/Arizona_State_Senate.

Balz, Dan, and Scott Clement. 2016. "Poll: Trump's Negatives among Hispanics Rise; Worst in GOP Field." *Washington Post*, February 25, 2016. https://www.washington post.com/news/politics/wp/2016/02/25/poll-trumps-negatives-among-hispanics -rise-worst-in-gop-field/.

Barreto, Matt. 2009. "Mobilization, Participation, and Solidaridad: Latino Participation in the 2006 Immigration Protest Rallies." *Urban Affairs Review* 44, no. 5: 736–64.

Barreto, Matt. 2013. "New Poll: Immigration Policy Stance Directly Tied to Winning the Latino Vote." Latino Decisions, March 5, 2013. http://www.latinodecisions .com/blog/2013/03/05/new-poll-immigration-policy-stance-directly-tied-to -winning-the-latino-vote/.

Bebout, Lee. 2016. *Whiteness on the Border: Mapping the U.S. Racial Imagination in Brown and White.* New York: New York University Press.

Beran, A. 2013. "Voting Rights Are Once Again Challenged at the Supreme Court." *Nation*, March 18, 2013. https://www.thenation.com/article/archive/voting-rights -are-once-again-challenged-supreme-court.

Berman, Ari. 2016. "There Are 868 Fewer Places to Vote in 2016 Because the Supreme Court Gutted the Voting Rights Act." *Nation*, November 4, 2016. https://www.the nation.com/article/archive/there-are-868-fewer-places-to-vote-in-2016-because -the-supreme-court-gutted-the-voting-rights-act/.

Biggers, Jeff. 2012. *State out of the Union: Arizona and the Final Showdown of the American Dream.* New York: Nation Books.

Billeaud, J. 2013. "Group Fails in Bid to Recall Ariz. Sheriff." Associated Press, May 30, 2013. https://apnews.com/article/2bdf00fbba3f42ccbd41d343508908db.

Boehm, Jessica. 2019. "Phoenix Raises Minimum Wage to $15 per Hour for City Employees." Arizona Central, April 4, 2019. https://www.azcentral.com/story/news/local /phoenix/2019/04/03/phoenix-raises-minimum-wage-15-per-hour-city-employees /3357465002/.

Bolick, Clint. 2008. *Mission Unaccomplished: The Misplaced Priorities of the Maricopa County Sheriff's Office.* Phoenix: Goldwater Institute.

Boone, Devin. 2019. "In This Swing State, Phoenix's Maricopa County Will Be the Battleground within the Battleground." *Prospect*, December 3, 2019. https:// prospect.org/politics/activists-work-overtime-to-turn-arizona-blue-2020/.

Briegel, Kaye Lynn. 1974. "Alianza Hispano-Americana, 1894–1965: A Mexican American Fraternal Insurance Society." PhD diss., University of Southern California.

Camarota, S. A. 2010. "Center for Immigration Studies on the New Arizona Immigration Law, SB1070." PR Newswire, April 29, 2010. https://cis.org/Center-Immigration -Studies-New-Arizona-Immigration-Law-SB1070.

Chávez, Leo. 2008. *The Latino Threat: Constructing Immigrants, Citizens, and the Nation.* Stanford, Calif.: Stanford University Press, 2008.

Chavez-Pringle, Jessica, Lavariega Monforti, and Michelle Michelson. 2015. *Living the Dream: New Immigration Policies and the Lives of Undocumented Latino Youth.* New York: Routledge.

Chicanos Por La Causa. n.d. "About Who We Are." Accessed November 16, 2020. https://www.cplc.org/about/about.php.

Ciment, James, and John Radzilowski. 2014. *American Immigration: An Encyclopedia of Political, Social, and Cultural Change*. 2nd ed. New York: Routledge.

CNN Wire Staff. 2010. "Shakira Enters Arizona Immigration Fight." CNN, April 30, 2010. https://www.cnn.com/2010/US/04/30/arizona.shakira.immigration/index.html.

Conroy, Scott. 2016. "Young Cuban Americans Think Marco Rubio Is Stuck in the Past." Huffington Post, March 14, 2016. http://www.huffingtonpost.com/entry/marco-rubio-young-cuban-americans_us_56e703f9e4b0860f99d9da34.

Cooperman, Alan. 2006. "Letter on Immigration Deepens Split among Evangelicals." *Washington Post*, April 5, 2006. https://www.washingtonpost.com/archive/politics/2006/04/05/letter-on-immigration-deepens-split-among-evangelicals/1b434c35-c776-447a-b26a-9fe3272369b7/.

Damore, David. 2016. "10 Reasons Why Immigration Politics Will Affect the Latino Vote." Latino Decisions, February 16, 2016. http://www.latinodecisions.com/blog/2016/02/16/10-reasons-why-immigration-politics-will-affect-the-latino-vote.

Danley, Ian. 2016. "Friends of Ian Danley." Accessed November 16, 2020. http://www.iandanley.com.

Department of Homeland Security. 2009. "Secretary Napolitano Announces New Agreement for State and Local Immigration Enforcement Partnerships and Adds 11 New Agreements." July 10, 2009. https://www.dhs.gov/news/2009/07/10/secretaryannounces-new-agreement-state-and-local-immigration-enforcement.

Díaz McConnell, Eileen, and Amanda Skeen. 2009. "Demographics: Contemporary Characteristics of a Dynamic Population." In *Looking Ahead (Viendo Adelante): The Past, Present, and Future of Hispanic Populations in the State of Arizona*. Tempe: Arizona State University/Arizona Latino Research Enterprise, Tempe, http://www.evanspubrelations.com/documents/StateofLatinoArizona_web_complete.pdf.

Dickson, Caitlin. 2013. "Sore Losers: 7 Juicy Bits from the GOP's Autopsy Report: Time for Some Tough Love—Republicans Leaders Have Dumped a 100-Page Report That Spells Out Why Their Party Is in Dire Straits." Daily Beast, March 18, 2013. https://www.thedailybeast.com/sore-losers-7-juicy-bits-from-the-gops-autopsy-report.

Donnelly, Robert. 2013. "State-Level Immigrant-Related Legislation: What It Means for the Immigration Policy Debate, Latino Politics, and Arizona's Immigration Law." In *Latino Politics and Arizona's Immigration Law SB 1070*, edited by Lisa Magaña and Erik Lee, 43–54. New York: Springer.

Finnegan, William. 2009. "Sheriff Joe Is Tough on Prisoners and Undocumented Immigrants. What about Crime?" *New Yorker*, July 13, 2009. https://www.newyorker.com/magazine/2009/07/20/sheriff-joe.

Fischer, Howard. 2016(a). "McCain Drops Trump Support Following Latest Controversy." Associated Press, October 9, 2016. https://apnews.com/eb97ad08623b4e7bae2aa6be7e80a5cf.

Fischer, Howard. 2016(b). "Restaurant Group Preps for Fight against Arizona Minimum Wage Boost." *Popular Democracy*, July 26, 2016. https://populardemocracy.org/news-and-publications/restaurant-group-preps-fight-against-ariz-minimum-wage-boost.

Gambino, L. 2016. "As Trump Slips into Red with Latinos, Democrats Hope to Turn Arizona Blue." *Guardian*, September 29, 2016. https://www.theguardian.com/us-news/2016/sep/19/donald-trump-arizona-latino-voters-democrats.

Gans, Judith. 2008. *Immigrants in Arizona: Fiscal and Economic Impacts*. Tucson: Udall Center for Studies in Public Policy.

García, Carlos. 2016. "My Turn: We Don't Have Luxury to Pick Battles." *Arizona Central*, April 18, 2016. http://www.azcentral.com/story/opinion/op-ed/2016/04/18/my-turn-we-dont-have-luxury-pick-battles/82798738/.

García, Mario, ed. 2014. *The Chicano Movement: Perspectives from the Twenty-First Century*. New York: Routledge.

Garcia Bedolla, Lisa. 2014. *Latino Politics*. Cambridge: Polity.

Gardiner, Dustin. 2018. "How Hobbs Won State's No. 2 Job." *Arizona Central*, November 29, 2018. https://www.azcentral.com/story/news/politics/elections/2018/11/16/katie-hobbs-apparent-winner-arizona-secretary-states-race-steve-gaynor/2029677002/.

Giles, Ben. 2019. "GOP Bill Would Restrict Vote by-Mail Options." *Arizona Capitol Times*, January 25, 2019. https://azcapitoltimes.com/news/2019/01/24/committee-approves-changes-to-voting-laws/.

Gómez-Quiñones, Juan, and Irene Vásquez. 2014. *Making Aztlán: Ideology and Culture of the Chicana and Chicano Movement, 1966–1977*. Albuquerque: University of New Mexico Press.

Gonzales, Alfonso. 2017. "Trumpism, Authoritarian Neoliberalism, and Subaltern Latina/o Politics." *Aztlán: A Journal of Chicano Studies* 42, no. 2 (Fall): 147–64.

González, Daniel. 2006. "Latino Leader Came to Forefront from Shadows." *Arizona Republic*, September 4, 2006. https://24ahead.com/latino-leader-came-forefront-shadows.

González, Daniel, Mel Meléndez, and Pat Flannery. 2006. "March of Strength/Over 100,000 Rally in Phoenix for Immigration Reform—Massive Crowds Highlight Economic, Political Might." *Arizona Republic*, April 11, 2006, n.p.

González, Daniel, and Yvonne Wingett. 2006. "Power of the Pulpit Inspired Immigrants to Protest." *Arizona Republic*, March 29, 2006, n.p.

Gordon, Linda. 2001. *The Great Arizona Orphan Abduction*. Cambridge, Mass.: Harvard University Press.

Gorman, Anna. 2010. "Jewish Group Denounces Comparisons of Arizona to Nazi Germany." *Los Angeles Times*, May 14, 2020. https://www.latimes.com/archives/la-xpm-2010-may-14-la-me-0514-arizona-wiesenthal-20100514-story.html.

Gorman, Anna, and Nicholas Riccardi. 2010. "Calls to Boycott Arizona Grow over New Immigration Law." *Los Angeles Times*, April 28, 2010. http://articles.latimes .com/2010/apr/28/local/la-me-0428-arizona-boycott-20100428.

Graber, N. 2017. "Do You Hear the People Sing? Theater and Theatricality in the Trump Campaign." *American Music* 35, no. 4: 435–45.

Gray, Laurel. 2011. "Latino Immigrants in South Phoenix: Perceptions of Health in Communities of Origin versus Communities in the United States." Honors thesis, Arizona State University.

Griffin, Rob, William H. Frey, and Ruy Teixeira. 2019. "States of Change." American Progress, June 27, 2019. https://www.americanprogress.org/issues/democracy /reports/2019/06/27/471487/states of-change-3/.

Gundran, Robert. 2018. "Proposals to Roll Back Arizona's Minimum-Wage Ballot Measure Protested at Capitol." Arizona Central, March 8, 2018. https://www.azcentral .com/story/news/politics/legislature/2018/03/08/proposals-roll-back-arizonas -minimum-wage-ballot-measure-protested-capitol/404302002/.

Hagan, J. 2012. "The Long, Lawless Ride of Sheriff Joe Arpaio." *Rolling Stone*, August 2, 2012. https://www.rollingstone.com/culture/culture-news/the-long-lawless-ride -of-sheriff-joe-arpaio-231455/.

Hardy-Fanta, Carole, and Jeffrey Gerson. 2002. *Latino Politics in Massachusetts: Struggles, Strategies, and Prospects*. New York: Routledge.

Hickson, Alessandra. 2013. "Thousands Rally for Immigration Reform in Nation's Capital, Legislators Arrested." NBC Latino, October 8, 2013. https://nbclatino.com /2013/10/08/caminoamericano-national-rally-for-immigration-reform-live-blog/.

Hidalgo, Edmundo. 2014. Personal conversation. Fall 2014.

Hing, Julianne. 2010. "Young People at the Front Lines of Pro-Migrant Movement, SB1070 Protests." Colorlines, April 23, 2010. http://www.colorlines.com/articles /young-people-front-lines-pro- migrant-movement-sb1070-protests.

Hoffer, A. L. 2017. "Donald Trump, How Did This Happen? An Analysis of Rhetorical Strategies Utilized in the 2016 Presidential Campaign of Donald Trump." PhD diss., Arizona State University.

Hudson, David. 2012. "The Top 5 Reasons Why SB 1070—and Laws Like It—Cause Economic Harm." Center for American Progress, June 25, 2012. https://www .americanprogress.org/issues/immigration/news/2012/06/25/11677/the-top-5 -reasons-why-s-b-1070-and-laws-like-it-cause-economic-harm/.

Jacobson, Louis. 2010. "The Majority of the People That Are Coming to Arizona and Trespassing Are Now Becoming Drug Mules." Politifact, June 30, 2010. https:// www.politifact.com/factchecks/2010/jun/30/jan-brewer/arizona-gov-brewer-says -majority-illegals-are-drug/.

Johnson, Jenna, Philip Bump, and Jose A. DelReal. 2016. "Protesters Block the Road to Donald Trump Rally near Phoenix." *Washington Post*, March 19, 2016. https://www.washingtonpost.com/politics/protesters-block-the-road-to

-donald-trump-rally-near-phoenix/2016/03/19/ed7f8e84-ed50–11e5-a6f3-21ccd bc5f74e_story.html.

Jordan, Miriam. 2016. "Arizona Sheriff Joe Arpaio Loses Bid for Seventh Term; Paul Penzone, Former Phoenix Police Sergeant, Will Lead Maricopa County Sheriff Department." *Wall Street Journal*, November 10, 2016. https://www.wsj.com /articles/arizona-sheriff-joe-arpaio-loses-bid-for-seventh-term-147866924.

Kasperkevic, Jana. 2012. "Deporting All of America's Illegal Immigrants Would Cost A Whopping $285 Billion." Business Insider, January 30, 2012. http://www .businessinsider.com/deporting-all-of-americas-illegal-immigrants-would-cost -a-whopping-285-billion-2012-1.

Kauffman, Gretel. 2016. "After Six Terms as Arizona's Enforcer Sheriff, Joe Arpaio Loses to Democrat." *Christian Science Monitor*, November 9, 2016. https://www .csmonitor.com/USA/2016/1109/After-six-terms-as-Arizona-s-enforcer-sheriff -Joe-Arpaio-loses-to-Democrat.

Kelsey, Adam. 2017. "Trump Pardons Controversial Former Arizona Sheriff Joe Arpaio." ABC News, August 25, 2017. https://abcnews.go.com/Politics/controversial-arizona -sheriff-joe-arpaio-pardoned-president-trump/story?id=49426093.

King, Jamilah. 2010. "Arpaio Arrests Dozens in SB 1070 Protests: Hundreds Take to the Streets in Arizona, and Beyond." Colorlines, July 30, 2010. http://www.color lines.com/articles/arpaio-arrests-dozens-sb-1070-protests.

Krogstad, Jens Manuel, Antonio Flores, and Mark Hugo López. 2018. "Key Takeaways about Latino Voters in the 2018 Midterm Elections." Pew Research Center, November 9, 2018. https://www.pewresearch.org/facttank/2018/11/09/how -latinos-voted-in-2018-midterms/.

Krogstad, Jens Manuel, Mark Hugo López, Gustavo López, Jeffrey S. Passel, and Eileen Patten. 2016. "Millennials Make Up Almost Half of Latino Eligible Voters in 2016 Youth, Naturalizations Drive Number of Hispanic Eligible Voters to Record 27.3 Million." Pew Research Center, January 19, 2016. https://www.pew research.org/hispanic/2016/01/19/millennials-make-up-almost-half-of-latino -eligible-voters-in-2016/.

Lacayo, A. Elena. 2011. "One Year Later: A Look at SB 1070 and Copycat Legislation." Isuu, April 18, 2011. https://issuu.com/nclr/docs/alookatsb1070v3.

Lachman, S. 2014. "Sheriff Joe Arpaio Considering a Run for Governor of Arizona." Huffington Post, January 23, 2014. https://www.huffpost.com/entry/joe-arpaio -governor-_n_4652851.

Lee, Kurtis. 2018. "Former Arizona Sheriff Joe Arpaio Is Back. So Too Are Latino Voters Who Helped Oust Him." *Los Angeles Times*, January 14, 2018. https://www .latimes.com/nation/la-na-pol-arpaio-latino-voters-20180114-story.html.

Lemon, Stephen. 2009. "Neo-Nazis and Extreme Right-Wingers Love Joe Arpaio, and There's Evidence That the MCSO Keeps Them Close." *Phoenix New Times*, May 14, 2009. https://www.phoenixnewtimes.com/news/neo-nazis-and-extreme

-right-wingers-love-joe-arpaio-and-theres-evidence-that-the-mcso-keeps-them
-close-6433053.

Levine, Daniel S. 2017. "Raúl Grijalva: 5 Fast Facts You Need to Know." Heavy, January 13, 2017. http://www.heavy.com/news/2017/01/raul-grijalva-donald-trump
-boycott-inauguration-arizona-bio-bernie-sanders-wife-family/.

Lilley, Sandra. 2015. "Hillary Clinton Taps DREAMer Lorrela Praeli As Latino Outreach Director." MSNBC, May 20, 2015. https://www.nbcnews.com/news/latino/hillary
-clinton-taps-dreamer-activist-lorella-praeli-latina-outreach-director-n361721.

López, Ashley, Bret Jaspers, and Sergio Martínez-Beltrán. 2019. "After Democrats Surged in 2018, Republican-Run States Eye New Curbs on Voting." National Public Radio, April 22, 2019. https://www.npr.org/2019/04/22/714950127/after
-democrats-surged-in-2018-republican-run-states-eye-new-curbs-on voting.

López, Gustavo, and Eileen Patten. 2015. "The Impact of Slowing Immigration: Foreign-Born Share Falls among 14 Largest U.S. Hispanic Origin Groups." Pew Research Center, September 15, 2015. http://www.pewhispanic.org/2015/09/15/the
-impact-of-slowing-immigration-foreign-born-share-falls-among-14-largest-us
-hispanic-origin-groups/.

Lopez, Michael. 2010. "Zack de la Rocha Explains the Sound Strike, More Artists Boycott AZ." *Phoenix New Times*, June 29, 2010. https://www.phoenixnewtimes.com/music
/zack-de-la-rocha-explains-the-sound-strike-more-artists-boycott-az-6615227.

Lord, Bob. 2015. "Citizens for a Better Arizona Leaves Us a Better Arizona." Blog for Arizona, February 28, 2015. https://blogforarizona.net/citizens-for-a-better
-arizona-leaves-us-a-better-arizona/.

"Luis Gutiérrez." n.d. Wikipedia. Accessed November 16, 2020. https://en.wikipedia
.org/wiki/Luis_Gutiérrez.

Macias, A. 2015. "Arizona's Demographic Gap Could Cause Political and Educational Issues." Frontera's Desk. Accessed November 18, 2020. https://fronteras
desk.org/content/102742/arizonas-demographic-gap-could-cause-political-and
-educational-issues.

Magaña, Lisa. 2014. *Arizona, Immigration, Latinos, and Politics*. Dubuque, Iowa: Kendall Hunt.

Magaña, Lisa. 2020. "Fear of Calling the Police: Regulation and Resistance." In *Social Welfare Policy: Regulation and Resistance among People of Color*, edited by Jerome H. Schiele, 255–70. Los Angeles: SAGE.

Magaña, Lisa. 2005. *Mexican Americans and the Politics of Diversity, ¡Querer es poder!* Tucson: University of Arizona Press.

Magaña, Lisa. 2013. "SB 1070 and Negative Social Constructions of Latino Immigrants in Arizona." *Aztlán* 38, no. 2 (2013): 151–61.

Magaña, Lisa, and Armando Xavier Mejia. 2004. *Latino Americans and Political Participation: A Reference Handbook*. Santa Barbara, Calif.: ABC CLIO.

Márquez, Ben. 2014. *Democratizing Texas Politics: Race, Identity, and Mexican American Empowerment, 1945–2002*. Austin: University of Texas Press.

McGreevy, Patrick. 2010. "Steinberg Says California Should Consider Boycotting Arizona in Protest of Immigration Law." *Los Angeles Times*, April 27, 2010. https://latimesblogs.latimes.com/california-politics/2010/04/darrell-steinberg-says-california-should-consider-boycotting-arizona-in-protest-of-immigration-law.html.

Meléndez, Mel, and Jim Hensley. 2006. "Students Call for Voice on Legal Status." *Arizona Republic*, April 8, 2006, n.p.

Mendoza, Jessica. 2016. "Rising Force in Latino Turnout: Hispanics Who Can't Vote." *Christian Science Monitor*, August 22, 2016. https://www.csmonitor.com/USA/Politics/2016/0822/Rising-force-in-Latino-turnout-Hispanics-who-can-t-vote.

Menjívar, Cecilia, and Lisa Magaña. 2005. "Immigration to Arizona: Diversity and Change." In *Arizona Hispanics: The Evolution of Influence*, edited by Louis Olivas, 53–71. Tempe: Arizona State University.

Mettler, Katie. 2019. "In Historic First, *Arizona Republic* Backs a Democrat for President, Citing Trump's 'Deep Character Flaws.'" *Washington Post*, April 30, 2019. https://www.washingtonpost.com/news/morningmix/wp/2016/09/28/for-first-time-ariz-republic-backs-democrat-for-president-citing-trumps-deep-character-flaws/.

Mohamed, Heather. 2017. *The New Americans? Immigration, Protest, and the Politics of Latino Identity*. Lawrence: University Press of Kansas.

Montini, E. J. 2017. "Donald Trump Pushes Arizona-style SB 1070 . . . on Steroids." *Arizona Republic*, August 8, 2017. http://www.azcentral.com/story/opinion/oped/ejmontini/2015/08/17/donald-trump-immigration-border-security-joe-arpaio russell-pearce-sb-1070/31837009/.

Montero, David. 2011. "Arizonans Oust Immigration Firebrand Russell Pearce: Enforcement Was Core Issue in Election Fight between 2 Mormons." *Salt Lake Tribune*, November 8, 2011. https://archive.sltrib.com/article.php?id=52873568&itype=CMSID.

Moodie-Hills, Aisha. 2019. "The Rise of the New American Majority." Harvard Kennedy School Institute of Politics. Accessed November 16, 2020. https://iop.harvard.edu/getinvolved/study-groups-0/spring-2019-aisha-moodie-mills.

Moore, Joan, and Harry Pachon. 1985. *Hispanics in the United States*. Upper Saddle River, N.J.: Prentice Hall.

Navarro, Armando. 2005. *Mexicano Political Experience in Occupied Aztlán: Struggles and Change*. Lanham, Md.: Altamira.

Newman Benjamin, Sono Shah, and Loren Collingwood. 2018. "Race, Place, and Building a Base: Latino Population Growth and the Nascent Trump Campaign for President." *Public Opinion Quarterly* 82, no. 1 (Spring): 122–34.

Noel, Linda. 2014. *Debating American Identity: Southwestern Statehood and Mexican Immigration*. Tucson: University of Arizona Press.

Nuño Pérez, Stephen. 2018. "Republican Anti-immigrant Ads, Messaging Can Drive Voter Attitudes." MSNBC, February 15, 2018. https://www.nbcnews.com/news/latino/republican-anti-immigrant-ads-messaging-can-drive-voter-attitudes-studies-n846251.

O'Dell, Rob, Yvonne W. Sánchez, and Caitlin McGlade. 2016. "Lack of Polling sites, Not Independents, Caused Maricopa Election Chaos." *Arizona Republic*, March 23, 2016. https://www.azcentral.com/story/news/politics/elections/2016/03/23/maricopa-county-presidential-primary-election-chaos-arizona/82174876/.

One Arizona. 2016. "Fact Sheet." Accessed November 16, 2020. https://onearizona.org.

One Arizona. n.d. "Member Organizations: Power of the People!" Accessed November 16, 2020. https://onearizona.org/member-organizations/.

One Arizona. 2020. "State of Latino Electorate." Accessed November 16, 2020. https://onearizona.org.

Pantoja, A., R. Ramírez, and G. Segura. 2001. "Citizens by Choice, Voters by Necessity: Patterns in Political Mobilization by Naturalized Latinos." *Political Research Quarterly* 54, no. 4 (December): 729–50.

Parraz, Randy. 2014. Personal conversation. Fall 2014.

Parrott, T., L. Kennedy, and C. Scott. 1998. "Noncitizens and the Supplemental Security Income Program." *Social Security Bulletin* 61, no. 4 (October 1998): 3–31.

Peterson, C. 1992. "Pioneer Settlements in Arizona." Brigham Young University. Accessed November 16, 2020. http://eom.byu.edu/index.php/Arizona,_Pioneer_Settlement.

Pérez, Ellie. 2016. Comments made in the course Arizona, Immigration, Latinos, and Politics, Spring 2016, Arizona State University.

Pew Research Center: Hispanic Trends. 2008. "Hispanics in the 2008 Election: Arizona." February 1, 2008. https://www.pewresearch.org/hispanic/2008/02/01/hispanics-in-the-2008-election-arizona/#fn-1497-1.

Pew Research Center: Hispanic Trends. 2011. "State of Latino Electorate." Accessed November 16, 2020. http://www.pewhispanic.org/states/state/az/.

Pew Research Center: Hispanic Trends. 2012a. "2010, Foreign-Born Population in the United States Statistical Portrait." February 21, 2012. https://www.pewresearch.org/hispanic/2012/02/21/2010-statistical-information-on-immigrants-in-united-states/#population-by-nativity-race-and-ethnicity-2010.

Pew Research Center: Hispanic Trends. 2012b. "2010, Hispanics in the United States Statistical Portrait." February 21, 2012. https://www.pewresearch.org/hispanic/2012/02/21/2010-statistical-information-on-hispanics-in-united-states/.

Pew Research Center: Hispanic Trends. 2016. "Millennials Make Up Almost Half of Latino Eligible Voters in 2016: Youth, Naturalizations Drive Number of Hispanic Eligible Voters to Record 27.3 Million." January 19, 2016. http://www.pewhispanic.org /2016/01/19/millennials-make-up-almost-half-of-latino-eligible-voters-in-2016/.

Pew Research Center: Hispanic Trends. 2020. "Census 2010." June 12, 2020. https:// www.pewresearch.org/hispanic/census-2010/.

Powers, Jeanne. 2013. "From Extralegal Segregation to Anti-immigrant Policy: Reflections on the Long History of Racial Discrimination and Colorblindness in Arizona." *Aztlán* 38, no. 2: 191–205.

Preston, Julia. 2016. "More Latinos Seek Citizenship to Vote against Trump." *New York Times*, March 7, 2016. https://www.nytimes.com/2016/03/08/us/trumps-rise-spurs -latino-immigrants-to-naturalize-to-vote-against-him.html?auth=linked-facebook.

Puente. n.d. "About Us." Accessed November 16, 2020. https://puenteaz.org/about-us/.

Ramos, Henry. 1998. *American GI Forum: In Pursuit of the Dream, 1948–1983*. Houston: Arte Público.

Riccardi, Nicholas. 2010. "Raul Grijalva's Win in Arizona Gives Liberals Something to Cheer." *Los Angeles Times*, November 4, 2010. www.latimes.com/archives/la -xpm-2010-nov-04-la-pn-grijalva-20101104-story.html.

Reifowitz, Ian. 2016. "2013 GOP: Need 'Welcoming, Inclusive Message' to Attract Hispanics. 2015 GOP: Trump Has Other Ideas." Huffington Post, August 10, 2015. http://www.huffingtonpost.com/ianreifowitz/2013-gop-need-welcoming-i_b _7967060.html.

Richomme, Olivier. 2017. "The Latino Vote: Toward More Polarization?" *Revue de recherche en civilization américaine*, no. 7: https://journals.openedition.org/rrca /826 (accessed November 16, 2020).

Robert Wood Johnson Foundation. 2014. "A Closer Look at Stress for Latinos." July 22, 2014. http://www.rwjf.org/en/culture-of-health/2014/07/a_closer_look _atcon.html.

Robles, T. 2017. Personal communication, April 13, 2017.

Rodríguez, Antonio, and Stella M. Rouse. 2012. "Look Who's Talking Now! Solidarity, Social Networks, and Latino Political Participation." Paper presented at American Politics workshop, University of Maryland.

Rosales, Arturo F. 1997. *Chicano! The History of the Mexican American Civil Rights Movement*. Houston: Arte Público.

Rosales, Steven. 2011. "Fighting the Peace at Home: Mexican American Veterans and the 1944 GI Bill of Rights." *Pacific Historical Review* 80, no. 4 (November): 597–627.

Rose, Joel. 2018. "Big Latino Turnout in Midterms Raises Stakes For 2020." National Public Radio, November 19, 2018. https://www.npr.org/2018/11/19/668665372/big -latino-turnout-in midterms-raises-stakes-for-2020.

Rosen, Ben. 2016. "Inspired by Trump, New Arizona Law Redefines Free Speech." *Christian Science Monitor*, May 17, 2016. https://www.csmonitor.com/USA/2016 /0517/Inspired-by-Trump-new-Arizona-law-redefines-free-speech.

Rucker, Philip. 2016. "The Trump Effect: Could Arizona Go Blue for the First Time in 20 Years?" *Washington Post*, June 18, 2016. https://www.washingtonpost.com /politics/the-trump-effect-could-arizona-go-blue-for-the-first-time-in-20-years /2016/06/18/a1ffe53e-34aa-11e6-8758-d58e76e11b12_story.html.

Ryman, Anne, and Daniel Gonzalez. 2017. "Arizona Appeals Court Overturns In-state Tuition for 'Dreamers.'" Arizona Central, June 20, 2017. https://www.azcentral .com/story/news/politics/arizona-education/2017/06/20/arizona-court-overturns -state-tuition-dreamers/412845001/.

Sampaio, Anna. 2015. *Terrorizing Latina/o Immigrants: Race, Gender, and Immigration Politics in the Age of Security*. Philadelphia: Temple University Press.

Sánchez, George. 1993. *Becoming Mexican American*. New York: Oxford University Press.

Sánchez, Nick. 2014. "GOP César Chávez: Former Republican Candidate Changes Name, Joins Dems." Newsmax, June 3, 2014. https://www.newsmax.com/TheWire /gop-cesar-chavez-ed-pastor-arizona/2014/06/03/id/574785/.

Santa Ana, Otto. 2002. *Brown Tide Rising*. Austin: University of Texas Press.

Santa Ana, Otto, and Celeste González de Bustamante. 2012. *Arizona Firestorm: Global Immigration Realities, National Media, and Provincial Politics*. New York: Rowman & Littlefield.

Santiago, Charlene. 2016. "Goodbye Arpaio, Hello Trump: How Do We 'Make America Great Again'?" *State Press*, November 10, 2016. https://www.statepress.com /article/2016/11/sp/opinion-how-do-we-make-america-great-again.

Santos, Fernanda. 2016. "Sheriff Joe Arpaio Loses Bid for 7th Term in Arizona." *New York Times*, November 9, 2016. https://www.nytimes.com/2016/11/09/us/joe -arpaio/arizonasheriff.html.

Santos, Fernanda, Juleanna Glover, Jeff Greenfield, and Alexandra Glorioso. 2019. "Joe Arpaio's Surprising Legacy in Arizona." Politico, November 10, 2019. https:// www.politico.com/magazine/story/2019/11/10/joe-arpaio-arizona-latino-activists -elected-office-229906.

Schneider, Anne, and Helen M. Ingram, eds. 2004. *Deserving and Entitled: Social Constructions and Public Policy*. Albany: State University of New York Press.

Scott, Eugene. 2016. "Former Arizona Gov. Jan Brewer Endorses Donald Trump." CNN, February 27, 2016. https://www.cnn.com/2016/02/27/politics/jan-brewer -donald-trump-immigration/index.html.

Sheridan, Thomas. 2012. *Arizona: A History*. Tucson: University of Arizona Press.

Shogren, Elizabeth. 2016. "In Arizona's Shift Toward Purple, a Backlash to Trump Hastens." *High Country News*, September 29, 2016. https://www.hcn.org/issues/48 .17/in-arizonas-shift-toward-purple-bigotry-and-vitriol-hasten-the-pace.

Southern Poverty Law Center. 2016. "Federation for American Immigration Reform." Accessed November 16, 2020. https://www.splcenter.org/fighting-hate/extremist -files/group/federation-american-immigration-reform.

Stern, Ray. 2013. "DREAMers Burn High School Diplomas at AG's Office to Protest College-Tuition Lawsuit." *Phoenix New Times*, October 29, 2013. https://www .phoenixnewtimes.com/news/dreamers-burn-high-school-diplomas-at-ags -office-to-protest-college-tuition-lawsuit-6643286.

Stuart, Elizabeth. 2019. "Arizona Workers 'Fight for $15.'" *Phoenix New Times*, November 5, 2019. https://www.phoenixnewtimes.com/news/arizona-workers -fight-for-15-7287284.

Smith, Dylan. 2011. "High Court Upholds AZ Employer Sanction Law." *Tucson Sentinel*, May 26, 2011. http://www.tucsonsentinel.com/local/report/052611_supreme court_everify/high-court-upholds-az-employer-sanction-law/.

S. R., M. 2018. "The Republicans Risk Imploding in Arizona." *Economist*, August 24, 2018. https://www.economist.com/democracyinameric/2018/08/24/the-republicans -risk-imploding-in arizona.

Stoll, David. 1990. *Is Latin America Turning Protestant? The Politics of Evangelical Growth*. Los Angeles: University of California Press.

Szkupinski-Quiroga, S., D. Medina, J. Glick, E. Aranda, C. Menjívar, and K. Donato. 2014. "In the Belly of the Beast: Effects of Anti-immigration Policy on Latino Community Members." *American Behavioral Scientist* 58, no. 13: 1723–42.

Tarnopolsky, C. 2017. "Melancholia and Mania on the Trump Campaign Trail." *Theory & Event* 20, no. 1: 100–28.

Teng, Sheree, and Tom K. Wong. 2016. "One Arizona: Evaluation Report." Unbound Philanthropy, Four Freedoms Fund, Phoenix, Arizona. Accessed November 18, 2020. https://fundingadvocacy.issuelab.org/resource/one-arizona-evaluation-.

Tobar, Héctor. 2016. "Can Latinos Swing Arizona? An Organization's Efforts to Get Out the Vote May Help to Determine Who Wins the 2016 Election." *New Yorker*, July 25, 2016. https://www.newyorker.com/magazine/2016/08/01/promise -arizona-and-the-power-of-the-latino-vote.

U.S. Census Bureau. 1990. "1990 Census Population General Population Characteristics Arizona." January 23, 2018. https://www2.census.gov/library/publications /decennial/1990/cp-1/cp-1-4.pdf.

U.S. Census Bureau. 2020. "Quickfacts." Accessed November 16, 2020. https://www .census.gov/quickfacts/AZ.

U.S. Citizenship and Immigration Services. 2018. "Consideration of Deferred Action for Childhood Arrivals (DACA)." February 14, 2018. https://www.uscis .gov/humanitarian/consideration-deferred-action-childhood-arrivals-daca.

U.S. Immigration and Customs Enforcement. 2020. "Immigration Enforcement: Delegation of Immigration Authority Section 287(g) Immigration and Nationality Act." June 19, 2020. https://www.ice.gov/287g.

"The Utah Compact." 2019. Utah Compact on Immigration, March 21, 2019. https:// www.theutahcompact.com/.

Vélez-Ibáñez, Carlos, and Elsie Szecsy. 2014. "Politics, Process, Culture, and Human Folly: Life among Arizonans and the Reality of a Transborder World." *Journal of Borderlands Studies* 29, no. 4 (November 2014): 405–17.

Vinopal, Courtney. 2020. "How Mexican American Voters Helped Turn Arizona Blue." PBS News Hour, November 4, 2020. https://www.pbs.org/newshour/politics /how-mexican-american-voters-helped-turn-arizona-blue.

Voter Participation Center. 2019. "The Rising American Electorate." Accessed November 17, 2020. https://archive.voterparticipation.org/our-mission/the-rising -american-electorate/.

Voter Participation Center. 2020. "Our Research." November 16, 2020. https://www .voterparticipation.org/our-research/.

Wagner, Dennis, and Tom Zoellner. 2001. "Arizona was Home to Bin Laden 'Sleeper Cell.'" *Arizona Republic*, September 28, 2001. https://s3.amazonaws.com/911time line/2001/arizonarepublic092801.html.

Weiner, Rachel. 2011. "Arizona Recall: Why Russell Pearce Lost." *Washington Post*, November 9, 2011. http://www.washingtonpost.com/blogs/the-fix/post/Arizona -recall-why-russel-pearce-lost/2011/11/09/glQALj6a5M_blog.html.

Wiltz, Teresa. 2015. "Racial Generation Gap Looms Large for States." Pew Charitable Trusts, January 16, 2015. www.pewtrusts.org/en/research-and-analysis/blogs/state line/2015/1/16/racial-generation-gap-looms-large-for-states.

Wood, Daniel. 2008. "Arizona's 'Virtual' Border Wall Gets a Reality Check: The Viability of a High-tech Barrier to Detect Illegal Border Crossers Remains Uncertain, after a Pilot Project Struggles." *Christian Science Monitor*, April 2, 2008. http://www.csmonitor.com/USA/2008/0402/p12s01-usgn.html.

Woodburry, Jason. 2012. "Rise Against Ends Boycott of Arizona." *Phoenix New Times*, May 18, 2012. http://www.phoenixnewtimes.com/music/rise-against-ends-boy cott-of-Arizona-sound-strike-changes-focus-6602726.

Woodruff, Betsy. 2016. "Requiem for a Republican Autopsy: After the 2012 Election Fiasco, the GOP Establishment Announced That the Party Must Change if It Was to Reach the Center Ground. Republican Primary Voters Have Responded—'No Way!'" Daily Beast, February 24, 2016. https://www.thedailybeast.com/requiem -for-a-republican-autopsy.

Wyloge, Evan. 2012. "Support for Sheriff Arpaio Declines Even in Some GOP Strong-holds." *Arizona Capitol Times*, December 20, 2012. https://azcapitoltimes.com/news/2012/12/20/arpaio-support-declines-even-in-some-republican-strongholds/.

INDEX

ABOUT THE AUTHORS

Lisa Magaña is a professor in the School of Transborder Studies at Arizona State University, where she has worked for more than two decades. She is the author of several books, including *Latino Politics and Arizona's Immigration Law SB 1070, Straddling the Border: The Immigration Policy Process and the INS*, and *Mexican Americans and the Politics of Diversity*.

César S. Silva received his PhD from the School of Transborder Studies at Arizona State University, specializing in Chicano/Latino public opinion and voter turnout, racial and ethnic identity in the United States, elections and campaigns, and Chicano/Latino public policy issues, with a focus on Spanish speakers.